iola is a Greek girls name that means 'violet dawn', and a Welsh name meaning 'valued by the Lord'.

Dear iola reader, you are dressed in royalty & treasured by God.

Scan to visit

© iola is published by abi louise roff
(formally abi partridge) abilouise.co

The Joy Issue. 7th issue of iola bookazine.
Published in November 2021. All rights reserved.
Photos licensed from Envato and Unsplash.

Our contributors are from all over the world.
Our spelling may differ but beneath the words
our hearts are leaning in the same direction.

Dear Reader,

Need a little silent night? Christmas season depleting your spirits a little? Tis' the season of joy but the pressure of the perfect celebrations, gifts, meals, homes, and conversations can get a bit too much.

If you don't want to lose the joy in the midst of it all – this issue is here to lighten your load. When you get a moment to put your feet up; remind yourself of your true joy, and all the little joys that make this time of year a delight. We can focus on the one from whom we draw our strength, in order to be strong for others. We *can* find our joy in the midst of seasonal stress.

If you love this issue do leave a review on Amazon there are issues for other seasons there too.

Now, your only decision is; coffee or hot chocolate?

Much love,

Abi

Writers in iola joy

In order of articles

Abi Louise

Monet Carpenter

Mary Mahan-Deatherage

Shay S. Mason

Noreen Sevret

Laura Rizkallah

iola * ISSUES

Other iola issues

Seasonally situated – always available. www.iolabookazine.com

Even in the Deep. MidWinter

Do you feel like you are in deep? Maybe you feel buried deep in a painful situation. Perhaps you have dreams that are buried deep. Maybe you have prayed that God would take you deeper but have no idea what that will look like.

Articles in this issue explore going deeper in times of transition, seeking hope in deep pain.

Perfect read for deep Winter, get your copy at iolabookazine.com.

Contributors include:
Kristin Vanderlip, Laura Thomas, Betsy Stretar, Sarah E Frazer Maria Dyck, Janine Dilger, Libby John

Articles; Buried dreams, Journal through the deep, And if not he is still good, Up from frozen ground, Awestruck, Wonderstruck, Lovestruck

The Fresh Issue. Spring

This issue reminds you God's mercies are new every morning and he is making all things new. It is fresh wind for when you are flailing, fresh flowers when desperate for beauty, fresh food for your soul, and fresh water for your thirst.

The fresh issue is a companion for your revitalisation.

Perfect read for Spring into Summer, get your copy at iolabookazine.com.

Contributors include:
Anna Kettle, Laura Thomas, Shay Mason, Melissa Smith, Sue Fulmore, Krista Hewlett, Jenny Sanders, Noreen Sevret, Jen Howard

Articles; Refections from a cherry tree, Soul spring clean, A breath of fresh air, Our daily bread, Washed by the water

The Rest issue. Summer

Struggle to find time to rest? Feel guilty for putting your feet up? The Rest issue leaves you feeling rested rather than agitated.

This issue makes your moment of peace the refreshment your soul needs. It provides a much-needed respite from the clamour of the world that we must do more, and be more.

Perfect read for high Summer, get your copy at iolabookazine.com.

Contributors include:
Kristin Vanderlip, Laura Thomas, Allison Craig, Tara Dickson, Shay S. Mason, Melissa Smith

Articles; Peace in safe places, Packing light, Letting the laundry wait, Rhythms of rest, Creativity and rest, An excerise in rest, Rest in motherhood

Contents

One Day *Abi Louise*	7
Joy Quotes	10
The wonder of expectation *Shay S Mason*	13
Colour & Pray *Deer*	16
Will he call me Dad? *Mary Mahan Deatherage*	17
Choose Joy *Colour, think & chat with Godventure*	21
Colour & Pray *Wreath*	23
Cookie cutter shaping *Noreen Sevret*	25
The healer of strivings *Monet Carpenter*	31
A view to breathe *St Magdalena,* *Trentino-Alto Adige, Italy*	34
Tidings of comfort and joy *Print*	36
Could-do list	37
Fill your cup	38
Joyful waiting *Mary Mahan Deatherage*	41
Dance in the kitchen *Print*	45
The snow under my feet **Journalling Prompts for the Winter Season** *Noreen Sevret*	47
Choose joy *Embroidery pattern from Tinkinstiches*	53
A tool to maximise joy *Mary Mahan Deatherage*	57

Light as a feather *Macrame feather wall hanging*	62
Joy playlist	64
Verses of Joy	65
Your Winter Joys *By Readers*	66
Get the party started *New Years conversation starters*	69
Book introductions	70
Bookmarks	73
A view to breathe *Hook Norton, Oxfordshire, UK*	74
The shape of joy *Abi Louise*	77
Celebrate *Decoration of Joy*	78
Plan with Purpose & Journal with Joy	81
Christmas Jewels *journal pages*	82
New Year Joys *journal pages*	85
Unexpected Joy *Laura Rizkallah*	87
Thank you notes	93
Go out with Joy *Blessing*	95

One day

Abi Louise

"*You can't not have brandy butter with Christmas Pudding,*" she exclaimed with a truly horrified tone! Sarcastically I suggested that "*Well, we'll just have turkey sandwiches instead for Christmas dinner*", which silenced her as she considered whether or not I was actually joking, I could see -"*I mean really, she wouldn't, would she?*"- scrolling through her mind.

Feeling under pressure with our mis-matched table and chairs, tiny kitchen and a hovering mother, Christmas was not feeling like the joyful day and dinner I was hoping for.

Why couldn't we serve dinner our own way? Why couldn't we just be on our own? Does anyone even like Christmas pudding or brussel sprouts? The burden of expectation and control, the stretch and release of parenting. The difference of values over food or meaning, tradition and holiday rest.

When I say I love Christmas, what I mean is, I love the run up to Christmas. Choosing gifts for loved ones that will delight them, the carols in churches by candlelight, the music in the shops, the twinkle lights and frosty mornings. The nativity plays where we wait with baited breath to hear whether one of the kings will give the baby Jesus "*frankenstein*" again, the shepherd's tea towel falling over their eyes and shy angels with tinsel halos. The wreath making, cookie baking and tree decorating. The Regent Street lights, the John Lewis TV Advert and the obscure perfume ones. The piles of Quality Street tins in the supermarkets, the scent of pine and mulled wine and cinnamon. The rich colours of red and green proving life is good and bountiful. This season is an aesthetic feast of beauty.

The actual day though? Once the stockings have been joyfully opened and the kids have run off with their new game, toy or chocolate I sit with a cup of coffee before facing the rest of the day, and feel a little deflated and tired.

The Christmas day church service consists of kids sharing their favourite gifts where parents resist feeling shamed for their extravagence or poverty. All-age services with challenges or team games - every introvert's nightmare. The home chefs distracted by whether they'd put the oven timer on or remembered the goose fat for the roast potatoes. You might get a free chocolate on the way out though.

Then we come to the dinner where something is always burnt or forgotten in the microwave, the kids don't eat their sprouts or swear in front of the grandparents, the merry uncle who starts *that* conversation and the weary mum's sarcastic comments let loose by the second glass of wine, and the oven door breaking!

Followed by the carnage of unrecyclable paper, ungrateful nephew and the in-law's enthusiastic dog knocking over the tree. Half the family loving the Queen's speech and her '*good Christian example*' and the other half muttering about class systems, Harry and Meghan, homelessness and palaces.

The expectation of perfection can spoil the celebration when reality bumps into it.

There's a whole season that leads to just one day. One day that wasn't meant to carry so much. Or does it echo the weight the first Christ's day carried? Unmet family expectations, hospitality fails, extravagent and curious gifts, misbehaving patriarchs*, the glory and the straw all seem to feature in the first story too.

One day I'll do it, do you want to come? I'm going to a cabin in the snow, somewhere like the rockies, I'm not cooking a turkey, we won't eat a brussel sprout, I'll bring the mince pies, (I won't have made them but they'll be from Marks and Spencer or Waitrose, I promise.) I'll leave the Christmas pudding and the brandy butter. We'll wear pyjamas and fluffy socks all day and won't leave the couch. I'll have a stack of books to share beside me, with a glass of mulled wine. We can eat cookies and popcorn and maybe a turkey, brie and cranberry sandwich from Pret or whatever Canada's version of Pret is.

When it gets dark I'll light candles and we can put everything down. We'll think about a girl about fourteen years old, identifying with her pain and elation of childbirth. Remembering how sorrow and joy can both exist at the same time. I'll whisper a thanks for her, the husband who didn't divorce her and the baby who definitely didn't eat turkey for dinner that day. I can almost smell that newborn baby scent. And if we listen closely we might hear the tinkle of chimes amongst the stars as the angels jostle for position to see and we'll know once more that all is well.

Ignore the probable actual timeline of King Herod's infanticide decree.

Abi Louise helps writers connect words with design so that it attracts and increases impact. She publishes iola bookazine and hunts for beauty between the beautiful Cotswolds and bookish city of Oxford where she lives with her three children. Find design for writers at abilouise.co

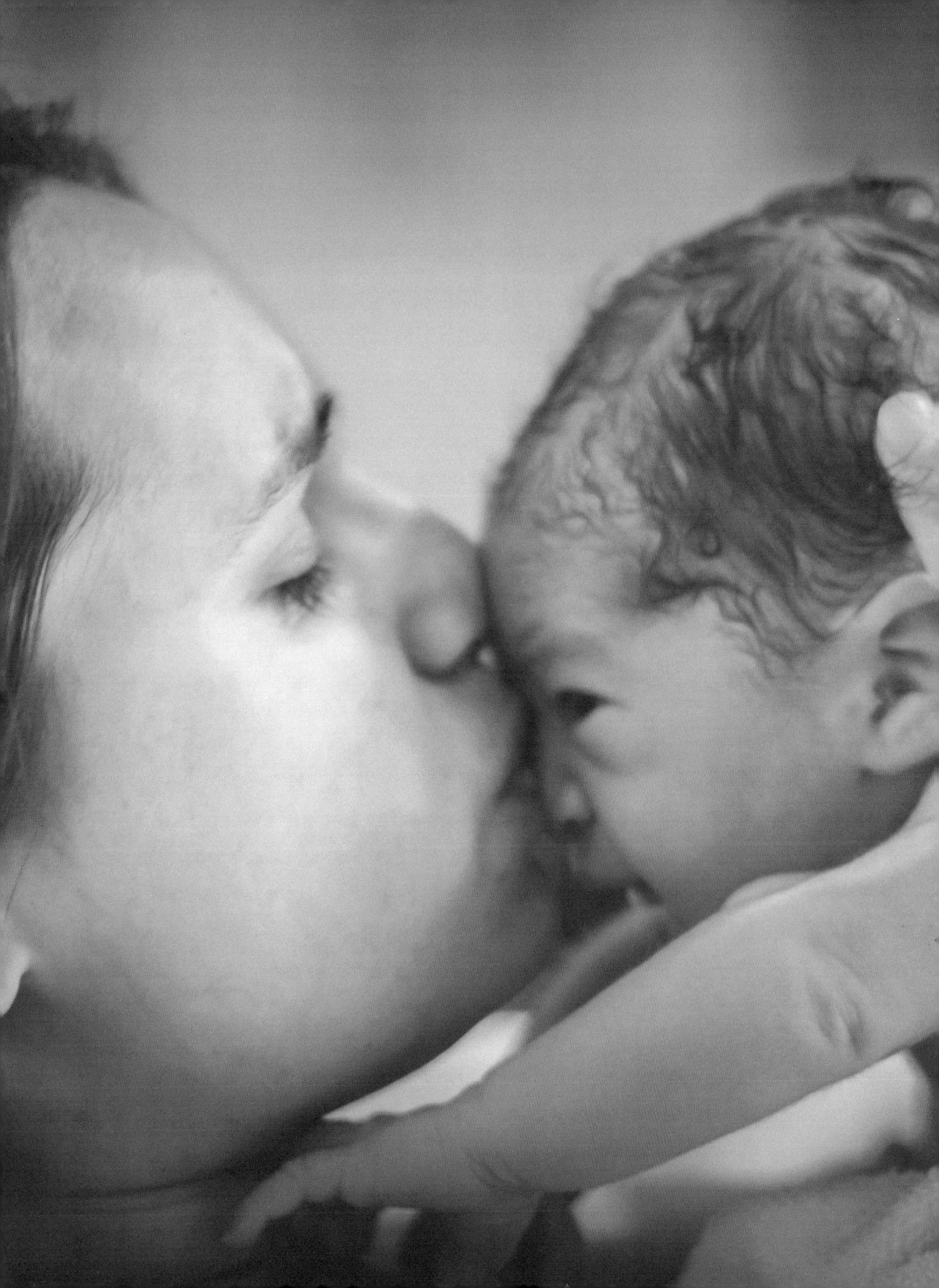

The wonder of expectation

Shay S Mason

Every good and perfect gift is from above, coming down from the Father of the heavenly lights, who does not change like shifting shadows. James 1:17

For many children, the Christmas season is filled with excitement and a sense of joyful anticipation. It was no different for me. I loved everything about Christmas. My family was a church on Christmas and Easter kind of family, and I didn't really know Jesus until I was 19, but I loved the beauty of the Christmas Eve service. It was special to be allowed to stay up late and wear a new dress. I remember stepping outside on a clear, cold Christmas Eve in Illinois and thinking the stars seemed especially bright. A thin layer of ice blanketed the driveway, and I was careful not to let my new patent leather shoes slip, even as my eyes were drawn toward the night sky. In that moment, my heart wanted to believe there was something magical about Christmas.

Each Christmas morning, I padded into the living room, taking in the glow of our colorful Christmas lights while inhaling the scent of fresh pine. Even the memory feels magical. What would be under the tree? There would surely be the gifts I had hinted to my parents I would like. But there would also be surprises I never anticipated. I especially relished the small wonders tucked inside my stocking. Perhaps some fancifully-shaped marzipan or mind-bending puzzle. What joy to be surprised!

The December I turned eleven I couldn't contain my excitement in the days leading up to Christmas. I decided I had to know what joys awaited. I stealthily searched every conceivable hiding place in our home. I found books and clothing, crafts and trinkets, games and gadgets. It was all delightful, and my anticipation grew. What other surprises would I discover on Christmas morning?

That year, I entered the living room with my usual anticipation. As an only child, the moment was all mine. In the early morning silence, I was free to unwrap everything under the tree. One by one, I unwrapped the gifts I had already seen hidden throughout the house. Surely there must be more? But there were no surprises to be found, not even in my stocking. As the reality hit me, I was overcome by a profound mixture of disappointment and shame. I knew the only person responsible for ruining my Christmas morning was me. My own impatience had stolen my joy.

Like many of life's disappointments, this was a lesson. Never again would I attempt to experience the wonder of Christmas morning before its proper time. I would learn to savor the wonder of expectation instead. And this lesson can be applied to every season of our lives. Like Mary, anticipating the birth of Jesus, our part is to trust that God will fulfill all things in their proper time. I wish I could so easily say, "*Let it be to me according to your word.*" (Luke 1:38)

But how often do we find ourselves trying to unwrap life's surprises before the proper time? We want to know what good things are headed our way. And sometimes our prayers reflect this restlessness. We ask God to reveal things we aren't yet ready to receive. We become impatient with God. Why? Perhaps we don't truly trust in his goodness. We aren't sure that what he has for us is what we really want. We want some assurance that life is headed in the direction we desire.

iola ★ JOY

There's no doubt life can be difficult to navigate at times. No one goes through life free from pain and struggle. People mistreat us. Tragedies happen. Our own human failings cause disappointment. In the midst of challenges, it is natural to want assurance that something better is around the corner. But the danger in rushing ahead is discovering we are no longer in tandem with God.

We have a Father who delights to "give good gifts" to his children (Matthew 7:11), but we often don't want to wait for his good gifts and attempt to take matters into our own hands. Just think of Sarah trying to fulfill God's promise of an heir by sending her servant Hagar to have a child with Abraham. God still blessed Sarah and Abraham with their own child, but Sarah's impatience had terrible consequences—especially for Hagar. (Genesis 16)

The world often whispers to us, Why wait? Get what you want now. Make your dream a reality. But how sweet it is to savor what God has for us in the moment, while still anticipating the good he has for us in the future. There is joy in the waiting, joy that we miss when we take matters into our own hands and ignore God's perfect timing.

In the last four years, my husband and I have heard at least five completely unrelated people say to us "God has something special right around the corner." The first time you hear it, you think "That's nice." The second time becomes, "That's interesting." By the third time you hear the same words, you begin to think, "God, what are you up to?" The last time someone said those words to us as she prayed, I actually bust out laughing. Not a cynical laugh, but a laugh filled with the joy of knowing her words were true.

This is the place where I continue to wait. I'm not going to try to charge around the metaphorical corner to see what's there. I have learned to trust more and more in his perfect timing. The joy of Christmas morning can't be rushed. In the meantime, I am savoring the wonder of expectation. That in itself is a gift.

Shay Mason is a Chicago-area native living in North Carolina. An auto-immune disease and OCD/anxiety overcomer, she is a firm believer in God's healing love. Her particular passion is helping people go deeper into God's heart. In addition to writing, Shay loves travel, music, coffee, quirky indie films, and hiking. Shay and her husband Bruce are the founders of Love Inside Out, Inc. in Raleigh and have spent extensive time ministering in Madagascar. They have two college-aged kids and a spoiled Goldendoodle. Shay is a contributor at She Found Joy and a member of Hope*Writers. Her blog The Spacious Place can be found at https://www.shaysmason.com.

Rest for the Weary is an invitation to give up the battle and surrender to the perfect love that casts out fear. Available on Amazon.

Colour and Pray

Then will the lame leap like a deer, and the mute tongue shout for joy. Water will gush forth in the wilderness and streams in the desert.

Isaiah 35: 6

Will he call me dad?

Mary Mathan Deatherage

It has been the craziest couple of weeks. But they fit perfectly with the insanity of the past few months. If hindsight is 20/20 then what is foresight? I could use a little of that right now.

Hmm... What to do ... what to *do*?

She's not feeling well. I've got to find a place for her to sit. Stay calm. My heart has been pounding out of my chest for weeks because of stress and worry. If I freak out, she will, too.

I'm trying to wrap my mind around the baby, plus this trip through the mountains. Why in the world are we doing this? This government is insane, although I'd never say that aloud. I can finally see the lights of Bethlehem. Thank you, God!

There are so many people here. This is ridiculous. I thought we'd easily find a place to stay. I just didn't think our plans through. We were in such a hurry. A friendly innkeeper offered the only solution when he saw how pregnant Mary was. Now, we have no choice but to sleep in a dirty cave. Mary says we'll be fine. She's sweet and calm. I'm sweaty and stunned. I'm such a failure. I had so much on my mind. I thought there would be more time. If we had left a couple of days earlier, I could've found a place for us to stay.

As I help Mary off the donkey, I roll the scene from a few months ago through my mind. It's kind of a never-ending loop. I attempt to pray it away every time it pops in my head ... which is a lot.

When I saw that she was pregnant, I was blown away. *Why* did this happen? *How* could this happen?

I must be insane because when she explained, I didn't believe her, but I did, too. The look on her face was so convincing.

I was angry. Then I was sad. I felt betrayed. How was there another man? I figured I'd just cancel the wedding quietly, not tell anyone. It's rough keeping the gossip mongers at bay, though. I love her. I just wasn't sure what to do. One thing I knew was that I couldn't let anything terrible happen to her.

Then I had the wildest dream. An angel came to tell me not to be afraid. Yeah, right. He revealed that she wasn't lying. Said I was chosen to protect them, to love them and to raise the boy. He said I could choose.

I cried.

I prayed.

I pulled my hair out.

I was sick and tired.

I decided to trust God.

What would you do?

When my friends asked about her, I told them, 'We're in love. That's all that matters. We're a team and the baby, *my* baby, will be cared for.' That mostly shut them up.

I hurried to prepare the house, our home, for Mary and our baby. Now we're hurrying because the government came up with this census thing. We've walked 90 miles this week, I'm exhausted. She's exhausted. I'm terrified because the baby is coming soon.

Oh no! The baby *is* coming! Mary is in pain, but she isn't screaming like I've heard other women do. I want to scream. I've never done anything like this before – that's what the midwives do. Lord, help me to know what to do. Also, Lord, forgive me for my ignorance and fear and help me to help her. Please keep us safe in this filthy place. Oh, why didn't I get us a room!

iola ⋆ JOY

She did it! I'm not sure how, but I prayed my head off. He's here! He's beautiful! He's *radiant*.

I'm amazed at how magnificent they both are. My heart is bursting with love. I'm praising God along with all these weird shepherds that are running around us wanting a peek at Him. Where did they come from?

I'm laughing. I'm crying. I'm exhausted.

Is that angels singing? I must be delirious.

Mary is resting. It's quiet now. Just the three of us plus a few cows and sheep huddled close to the fire. We're all keeping Him warm. As terrified as I am, I'm thanking God over and over for this miracle. God asked me to trust Him. I did. This whole thing is amazing. Awe inspiring, really.

What a huge responsibility. Will I have enough money to provide for Him? Will I be able to teach Him anything? Am I up to the task? I hope so. Do I have to change diapers? I hope not.

As I look at this beautiful baby's face, I am overwhelmed with love. I see His radiance all around us and the glow on Mary's face. My faith is in God. I know He will protect me while I protect this beautiful little family. I'm going to be the best father ever. I'll love Mary and Jesus until the day I die … forever.

I can't fathom that this baby is the Savior of the World, but God told us that He is.

We're gonna take this one moment at a time.

I wonder if He'll call me Dad.

Mary Mahan-Deatherage is a freelance writer, brand designer and strategic planner.

MMD Creative is her flagship company specializing in branding and strategic planning for small businesses. She owns *Spoken Women*, a creative community bringing the Catholic perspective to the world through bold writing, podcasts, and art. Her blog, *Divine, Clever, or Whatever* is a Christ-driven endeavor to lighten your soul through her uplifting stories. Mary is a mom of two and Mimi to a pair of rambunctious grandsons. She and her husband, Greg, are enjoying their vibrant, amusing, busy empty-nester life in Dixon, Illinois in the 127-year-old Craftsman home where she grew up. mmd-creative.com, spokenwomen.com, divinecleverorwhatever.com

iola ★ JOY

Choose Joy

Overleaf is a poster for you or your children to colour.

What brings you joy? How can you choose joy?

Think or chat about this as you colour this poster.

Put it up somewhere to remind you to choose joy!

You could combine colouring with something else which brings you joy (#doublejoyfix). Here's some ideas:

- a cup of nice tea
- sharing it with someone you like spending time with
- burning a nice candle or essential oils
- playing music or an audio book or podcast you enjoy

This poster is a resource from Godventure. Godventure exists to bring resources to families to explore faith together at home. From advent sticker calendars to mini-mags, and focusing on families with children from the ages of 3-10 you can find out more at godventure.co.uk

GodVenture

Colour, think & chat

Colour & pray

Cookie Cutter Shaping

Noreen Sevret

The mixing bowls and spoons line the space where flour has also made its appearance on the counter, on my apron, and even some on the floor at my feet. The dough is laid out thin on the counter before me, keeping the Christmas tradition alive for another year. The rolling pin speaks of having been in use after the rolling out of the dough, with small pieces of dough still clinging to its rounded edges. The evidence of cookie cutters are seen in the dough in various places where the shapes are now empty and cookies have been cut out of the puzzle of dough in front of me. The sound of the timer goes off, reminding me to take a peek inside the window of my stove to see how the cookies are baking. They look like they are almost, but not quite, done. The baking time of 10 minutes cannot be rushed. I have to slow myself and wait as they slowly cook in the heat of the oven. Familiar shapes line the trays as the Christmas cookies bake in shapes I've chosen, including Christmas trees, snowflakes, stars, bells, gingerbread men, candy canes, ornaments, and a snowman. After I take them out of the oven, I carefully remove them from the cookie tray one by one to cool before coloring them with sweet homemade frosting in pastel colors of pink, green, and blue.

The frosting is made using just the right ingredients, including the flavor of vanilla, anise, or peppermint. I use a simple butter knife to frost my cookies with much care, making sure to cover them without going over the edges, because going over the edges means I must eat a sample of them which I really enjoy doing! My favorite part of making these cookies, I think, is frosting them. It makes me think of my grandmother, who always used to make cut-out Christmas cookies at holiday times. Oh how I loved to eat her cookies! They always were delightfully delicious and never browned or burnt like mine occasionally get. My memories are filled with times when as a young girl I spent time with her in a toasty warm little kitchen and watched as she baked. She amazed me by the way she baked and how much I felt loved in her presence. I miss my grandmother, but the love she had for me was something that shaped my life, just like the cookie cutters shaped the cookies baking in the oven.

As I continue the process of cutting out cookies, baking them, cooling them, and then frosting them, I savor the way they smell and taste. When they are cooling on the tray, I notice across the counter a cookie that didn't get baked and got forgotten in the dough. I turn my stove back on and bake the one last cookie while I am cleaning up everything else. At the end of the long evening, with flour still covering parts of me that shouldn't be covered with flour, I make myself a cup of hot cappuccino piled with whipped cream and delight in the way my freshly baked cookies taste. As I sit down to write, and look across at all of my cookies, I think about how we are all somehow a little bit like the Christmas cookie that is cut out of the dough and laid out thin in a special shape.

I may not delight in the shape I find myself in, but it was a shape that was chosen and formed in my mother's womb by God Himself, who "made all the delicate, inner parts of my body and knit me together in my mother's womb." Psalm 139 says that we are all made wonderfully complex, that God saw us before we were born (vs. 16), and that before a single day of our life had passed, every moment was laid out and every day recorded in His book (vs. 16). God alone determined our shape, where we would be born, and chose us to each be woven together in the womb. It is a truly beautiful thing. He chose the womb as the place of shaping — the place where we are each knit together. He also chose the womb of a teenage girl named Mary as the place of shaping for His precious son, Jesus, as she gave birth to Him and laid Him in a manger that day long ago. We celebrate Jesus' birth on Christmas Day each year, even though it is not the exact date he was born. I believe just as I chose the shape of my cookies, He chose the "shape" for me; not just a physical shape but the shaping of who I am inside — what I take delight in, what I am passionate about, what moves me to tears, what causes me to go out of my way to care for others, what I delight in regarding the work I do, how I love those entrusted to my care, whether I love cookies or cake, whether I enjoy walking or running, and a million other things that make up who I am and who you are!

There are times when you may feel much like the Christmas cookie who has been dropped, broken, burnt, or left in the dough laid out thin, forgotten, and lonely. It is during those times Jesus wants you to know that even though you may feel that way in this broken world we live in, He has not forgotten you. He came for you the night He was placed in a manger. He knows everything about you — when you sit down or stand up and your every thought when far away (Ps. 139:1-2). He desires to heal that which is broken inside you and those places that hurt.

The frosting on the cookie is a lot like His love ~ spread out covering us right up to the edges of who we are and what we walk through, reaching out to us in the deepest part of our pain and in that place where we feel so alone. No matter where we find ourselves, we all are frosted by His love and grace that cleanses us from every sin (I John 1:7). Just like the frosting can be made in different flavors, I think there are different flavors to God's love for us. His sacrificial love came as One born in a manger, Immanuel, meaning God is with us. His saving love came on the cross as He died for us. His ever present love still is with us when we wake up in the morning (Ps. 139:18). His artistic and faithful love is evidenced by the sunsets and sunrises that faithfully remind us of who He is. His Word, the Bible, is a gift of love that reaches deep into us as we read the words and seek to know Him. His love that holds takes us when we are breaking and holds us together in ways only He can do. His deep love for us covers a multitude of our sins. His everlasting love for us never fails.

The season of Advent is a season of waiting and anticipation. In other seasons we wait as well, like waiting for the New Year and for the winter season to be over! We don't like to wait, but just like we have to wait for cookies to bake, we wait in this season as well. We set the timer and then wait. We pray for certain things and then wait. We parent our children and then wait to see the fruit of that season. We buy presents, then wait for the celebration for them to be opened. Mary was told she would give birth to Jesus, and then she had to wait.

iola ✶ JOY

So as we enter this season and time of waiting, let us set our timers so the cutout cookies we have shaped do not burn. Let us lift our eyes to Him, remembering how preciously shaped by God each one of us is, including those we dearly love and the strangers whose paths we cross in daily life. Let us wait quietly in moments when we are troubled, anxious, or feel lonely, knowing the One who shaped us in the beginning, sees us in that "place in the dough of life". Just like we do with making cookies, we can trust Him to lift us out of that place and re-shape what He made because He has great purposes for us. Let's seek Him with an open heart and give thanks for His love that came on that long ago day. His love fills those who open their hearts to Him.

Noreen Sevret lives on a picturesque river in Upstate New York with her husband and their son. She has a passion for finding beauty in unexpected places from behind the lens of her camera and writing about how God speaks to her heart through that picture. She facilitates journaling classes at her church. Noreen enjoys spending time with family, writing worship songs, playing the piano, reading, participating on book launch teams, going out for coffee with friends, and going to beautiful places in NYS and beaches in NJ with her husband. She also works as an office manager for a local funeral home. www.noreensevret.com IG: @writerbytheriver.

The healer of strivings

Monet Carpenter

You have permission to sit down.

Yes, you. Right now.

I know, I know, you can't. The lists won't accomplish themselves, the kids are bored and bickering, and it's time to make your famous dish for the umpteenth gathering marking up your calendar this month.

But you see, when we forfeit the opportunity to cease striving, our physical bodies suffer. The pressures to beat the clock will undoubtedly cause stress hormones to elevate our heart rate, inhibit our subconscious ability to breathe slowly and deeply, slow down our gut's ability to extract precious nutrients and trigger our muscles to be on the ready and tense.

And so, for the time being, find your spot, park yourself in it, and breathe.

I make myself do this often, forcing myself to sit. I recently discovered that I'm really good at allowing my work to steal my joy, disrupt my hope, and impede my intimacy with Christ. The not-so-funny thing is, I only discovered this truth *after* I gave myself a time out.

In my head, it's very easy for me to argue the lie 'If I'm not productive, then have I truly earned the right to sit at all?' I know my thinking is flawed. What's more, I know the enemy would like nothing more than to run me into the ground at the hands of my constant toiling.

But God intended our efforts to produce for us a fruit capable of yielding much more than scratched-off lists and satisfied engagements.

As a matter of fact, He's gone to extreme lengths on our behalf just to make it so.

Abandon your work for intimacy with Christ

When we abide in Christ, our toils become less demanding, and transform into pleasant offerings of love. Our hearts swell as we breathe in quiet, stillness and peace in order to propel us forward in our acts of service. When God defines our work and worth it yields intimacy with him. When we find ourselves spinning our wheels, exhausting our hearts, or weighted down by worry, fleeing our work to sit and worship will always draw Jesus near.

"Remain in me, and I in you. Just as a branch is unable to produce fruit by itself unless it remains on the vine, neither can you unless you remain in me. I am the vine; you are the branches. The one who remains in me and I in him produces much fruit, because you can do nothing without me."
John 15:4–5 CSB

Thankfully for us, there is no good work we can accomplish outside of intimacy with Christ. This means the pressure's off us. We have Jesus' permission to slow down, seek stillness, and surrender our toilings to him.

Searching for joy in the comfort of Christ

As we lean more fully into our abiding, stripping off the relentless layers of hustle and hurry, we uncover a newfound radiance bursting forth within us. When all we know is the comfort of Christ, all we desire becomes clear.

And yet, the realities of life are still upon us.

We will indeed glean nourishment in our moments of rejoicing and worship but we will also feel

iola ★ JOY

overwhelmed as we face the alluring festivities of the season: sorting through dozens of matching Christmas pjs, baking sweet treats to serve aside a delicious peppermint hot chocolate, or making our way to the best orchestrated light show in town.

We cannot escape the world, but we can cling to the comfort Christ brings. There is no greater elation than when we choose to make Christ the center of all our pursuits. Maybe, this year, it'll look like sneaking away with some of that piping hot, hot chocolate, and sitting outside bundled up alone to be filled by the stillness the cold air often brings.

And then, we can delight in Jesus, our joy in comfort.

Emmanuel, our long-awaited hope

When we've stolen ourselves away to abide more deeply, re-ignited by the joy such comfort brings, we finally find ourselves in the glorious presence of Emmanual, God with us.

Here, the glitterings of our toils diminish, our strivings become stunted and our hearts explode in wonder. For here, in this sacred space, our hope is made real. In our newfound absence of chaos, we draw near to the triumphant victory awaiting us.

God has given us the gift of Christ, and through him our hope is made secure. Isaiah 9:6 points our hearts to what is true and tangible:

"For a child will be born for us, a son will be given to us, and the government will be on his shoulders. He will be named Wonderful Counselor, Mighty God, Eternal Father, Prince of Peace." CSB

Rejoicing in the day to day

Our eyes and ears are constantly thrusting us into process mode. What we see starts the running list of what still needs to be cleaned, fixed up, or handled. Our ears are attuned to the demands of our family, the fight that needs refereeing, or the phone that won't stop dinging.

And in our attempt to satisfy all the pressing demands, we find ourselves fatigued, grumpy, and flat. We start doing and neglect being.

Today, at this moment, we can choose a reset. We get to decide our where, when, and how. Where will we meet with Christ, when will we make it happen, and how will we adapt our day to fit our most sacred need?

Monet lives in Alabama with her best friend and husband, Josh. Together they're raising two kiddos in a house full of lots of noise, crumbs, and many baskets of clean, but unfolded laundry. Monet lives the messy, unspoken parts of life openly to encourage other women that they too can embrace wholeness despite brokenness.

https://livingandlovingwhole.com/
IG: @monet.carpenter
Free resource: https://marvelous-architect-5399.ck.page/af7603c696

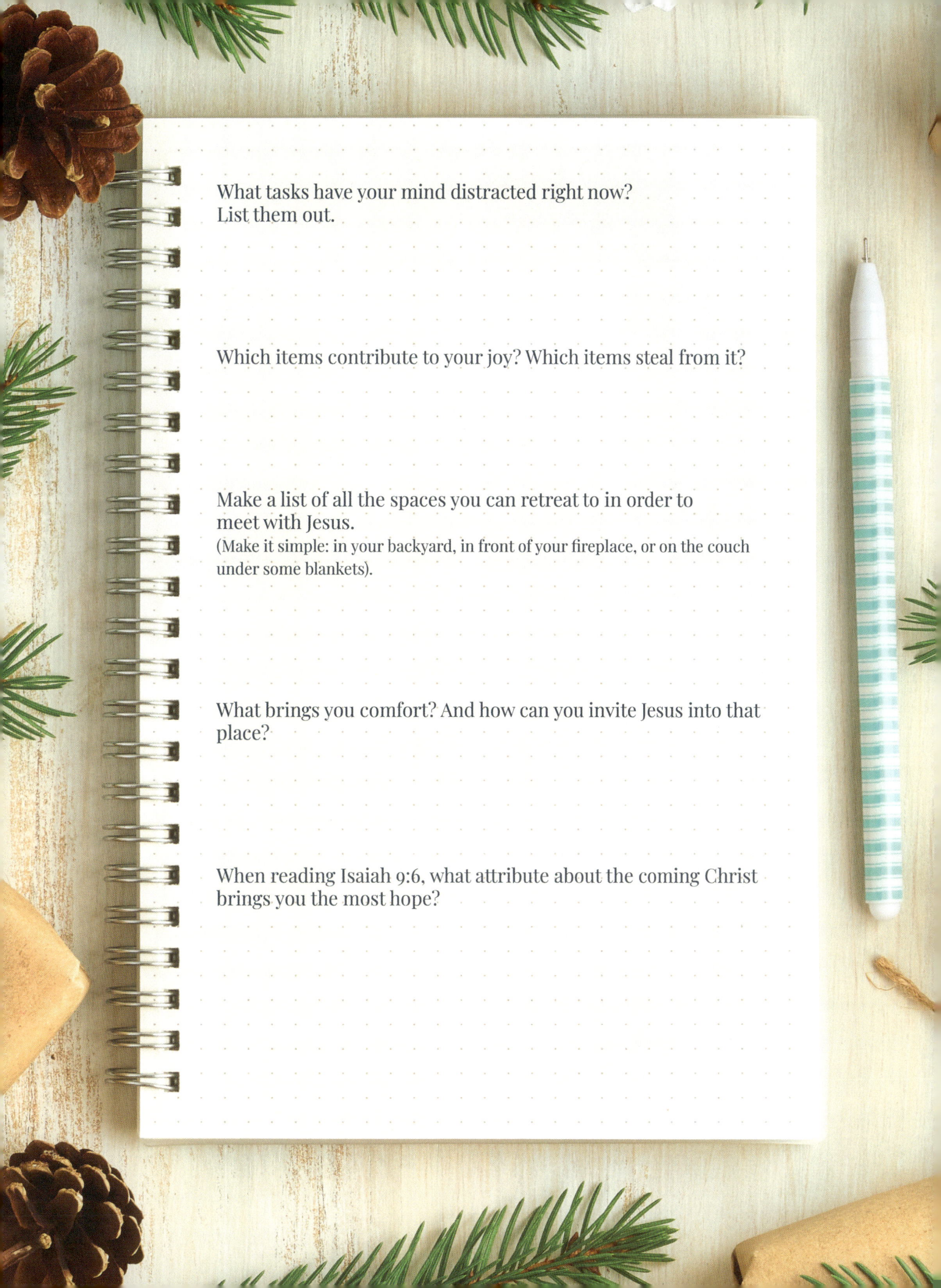

What tasks have your mind distracted right now? List them out.

Which items contribute to your joy? Which items steal from it?

Make a list of all the spaces you can retreat to in order to meet with Jesus.
(Make it simple: in your backyard, in front of your fireplace, or on the couch under some blankets).

What brings you comfort? And how can you invite Jesus into that place?

When reading Isaiah 9:6, what attribute about the coming Christ brings you the most hope?

Could-do list

Take a drive after dark with the kids to see the Christmas lights in your neighbourhood, in pyjamas, with hot chocolate in travel mugs, popcorn and Christmas music playing.

Sing carols at your neighbours doors and hand out Christmas cookies or mince pies.

Take a photo walk to hunt for winter beauty in nature.

Give something special to the food bank.

Light your candles and turn off the lights.

Cut some evergreen branches and fill vases in your house.

Place sugar in the bottom of an empty jar and add little trees, houses, animals or cars for a little wintry scene.

Make a list of seasonal themed books to read in between Christmas and New Year.

Celebrate the 12 days of Christmas by making a post-advent calendar of things that will bring you joy each month of the coming year.

Fill your cup

Cardamon Coffee

a few Cardamon pods
(5 pods for about 3tbsp of ground coffee)
ground coffee

If you have a coffee grinder, place spices in with your beans and grind. If not grind Cardamon pods with a pestle and mortar and add to your favourite coffee blend.

Make coffee as usual in your cafetiere or espresso machine.

Nutmeg & Orange Christmas Coffee

4 tbsp ground coffee
1 small cinnamon stick
2 pitted dates
pinch of ground nutmeg
2 cloves
strip of pared orange zest

Put the ground coffee, cinnamon stick and dates in a large cafetiere. Add the ground nutmeg, cloves and orange zest, then pour freshly boiled water over.

Stir gently with a wooden spoon, then leave to steep for 4 mins. Slowly push down the plunger and serve in espresso cups.

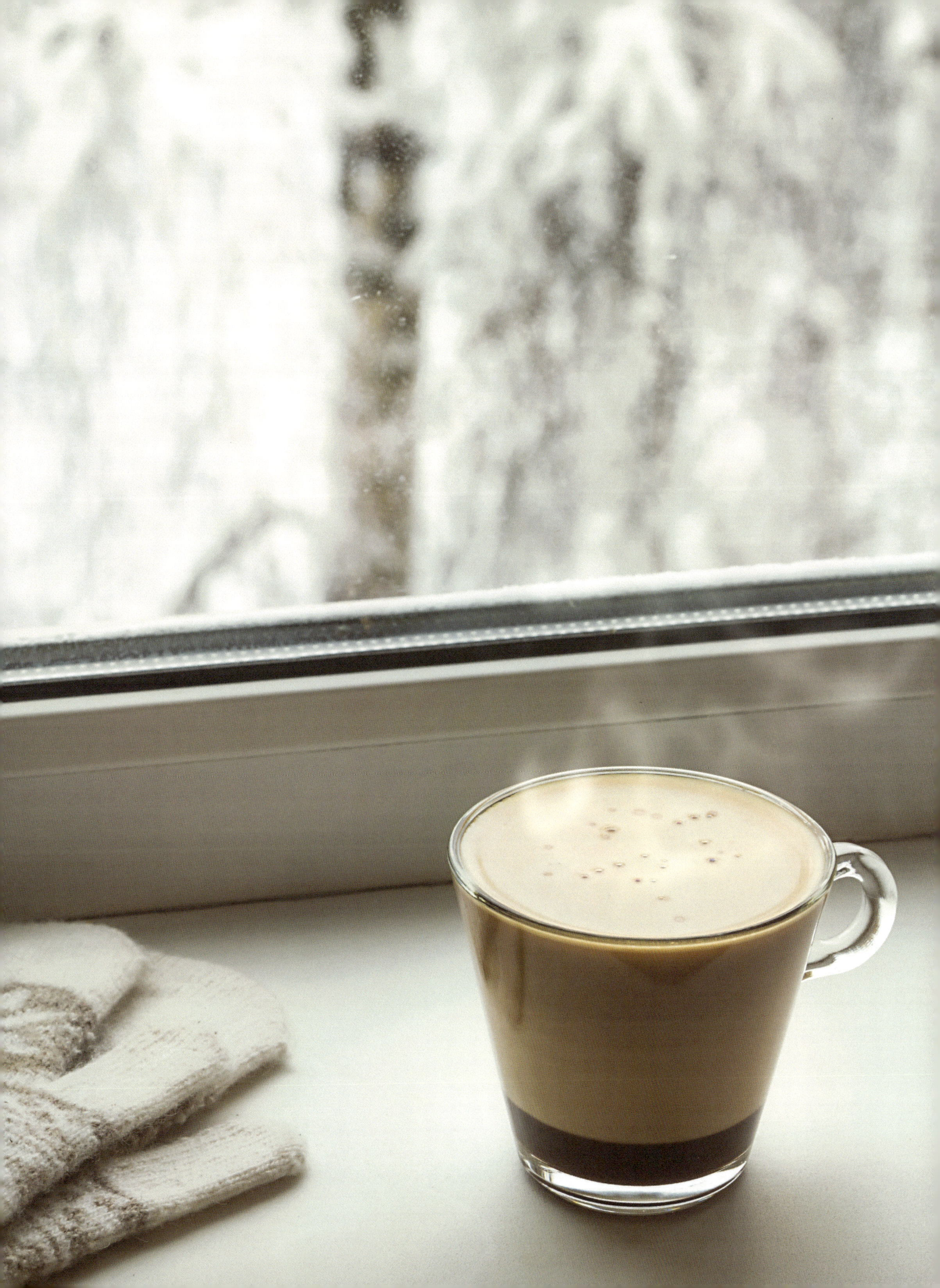

Mary Mahan-Deatherage

Joyful Waiting

Mary Mahan-Deatherage

Yom Yahveh - Day of Perfect Being

I have achieved a peaceful life. I've learned to savor most every moment of every day. This peace doesn't come easy. But it's a practice I've grown to love, so I work at it.

Recently, while reading ways to honor my weekly vacation day, Sunday, I ran across a phrase I'm unfamiliar with: *Yom Yahveh*. I learned this Jewish phrase has two meanings: *Day of the Lord* or *Day of Perfect Being*. In our modern world, most of us understand Sunday is the Lord's Day. But I became intrigued by the second meaning of the Day of Perfect Being.

Simply put, it's a practice focusing on just being in the here and now. No worries. Joyful waiting. You may recall Psalm 46:11 *"Be still and know that I am God! I am exalted among the nations, exalted on the earth."* One of the most popular verses across Christianity, it encompasses that concept of a Day of Perfect Being.

So, how does a Day of Perfect Being happen? Choose your day. It could be Sunday but with busy lives and varied work schedules Sunday may not work for you. Then, for your entire day purposefully let go of all that has happened in your past. Set aside all that may happen to you in the future. Stay in the moment and let God be God.

Impossible! I thought so. I've spent years wishing days away – wishing even seasons away.

"The weather is too hot this summer! I wish it was fall."

"Too much snow this winter; I wish spring would hurry and get here."

And on and on and in an endless loop. Then I'd add on every event of my life. It started when I was a child.

"I can't wait until I'm in high school … college … married … the baby comes … I get that new job …"

It's not that I wasn't grateful for all the good blessings and people in my life. My younger self was constantly striving because that's what our culture taught us to do. Nothing wrong with striving. It's noble and good and God wants us to do good works in the world. It's the constant, endless striving that steals your peace. It's missing being in the moment.

For instance, while feeding your baby you're mindlessly running through the laundry and house cleaning chores that are left undone. It's toiling on a work project and fretting about the fun you're missing with your kids. It's being at a family get together and worrying about that undone work project. And the big one – writing your grocery list in your mind while making love.

I've done it all. Embarrassingly, especially the last one. I think I need to apologize to my husband.

We've read countless articles touting the wonders of living in the moment. Why is this one different? Well sister, for me it all came to a crashing halt a few years ago when my husband suffered a cardiac arrest after mowing our lawn. Just a regular, warm Friday afternoon, just a healthy guy living his best life, just a mundane chore, just a moment in time that hit me like a cannonball.

God uses whatever he needs to open our eyes. There's a purpose for each event big and small, tragic, or joyful. We just need to take the time to see, to listen, to hear His whisper or maybe feel His thunder.

I felt God's thunder that sunny summer afternoon. I had no choice. God has always been a partner in my life, and I had let Him slip into the background with my busyness. He found a way to bring me back to Him and He'll find a way for you, too.

The Day of Perfect Being is a good place to start. One question I wondered, 'Is constantly living in the moment reckless at best – irresponsible at least?'

It can be!

Another question I wrestled with, 'How do I run my life without planning what's for dinner?'

We're not abandoning our responsibilities here. Plan your meals. Manage your life. We're looking at the big picture. It's not meant to add to your stress. Baby steps. Start with one day – your Fun day.

If you are dissatisfied with your season of life right now here are a few ways that might help relieve some stress and, with practice, aid in achieving a bit of peace.

First, identify the season you are in as opposed to the season you want to be in. Watch for and enjoy the blessings of the current season while you're working toward the next. Appreciate what's happening now and don't worry too much about the later.

Second, be patient. Recognize the fact that you're growing, we're all growing, no matter our age.

Ask yourself, 'How do I want to continue my life in a way that feels like a total place of joy?'

Third, be active. Do the work of the day. Then, pose the question, 'What are the things I need to be working on in my life so I can be that great mom, employee, friend, artist, writer, wife.

More importantly, ask, 'What do I want this one gorgeous life to be like on a day-to-day basis?'

Finally, have awareness of God in the present moment. God is communicating His light, His holiness, His grace right now! To be holy is to be present to God's will.

Ask God, 'What is the best thing for me today?'

Then listen. Start with an open mind. Start with tiny steps. Even a smidgen of stillness with God has benefits.

Ways to practise your Day of Perfect Being? Look at your baby while feeding her and feel her joy. Thank God for her and ask for the strength to be the best mom you can be. Or commit energy into your work projects. Find a way to enjoy them whether your job feeds your soul or is simply a stepping stone to feed your kids. If your family is a joy to be around or a thorn in your side, be in the moment and try to see what God is teaching you in that situation.

It's the voices of fear and scarcity and striving that may have you wanting to hold on to things or thinking you need to keep everything balanced or handled or you're going to lose. If you find yourself in an obsessive loop of planning or rethinking every decision, ask Him to see what He saw on that first Sabbath day when He rested. You'll be surprised at the answer.

Do I worry? Definitely. But I don't worry often. Do I strive – you betcha! I have goals and plans and God is right there with me in those plans. But offering Him my life has made all the difference in my sanity and peace. Staying in and being grateful for today has blessed me with a clear understanding of what matters most.

My go-to scripture is the tried-and-true Philippians 4:6-7:

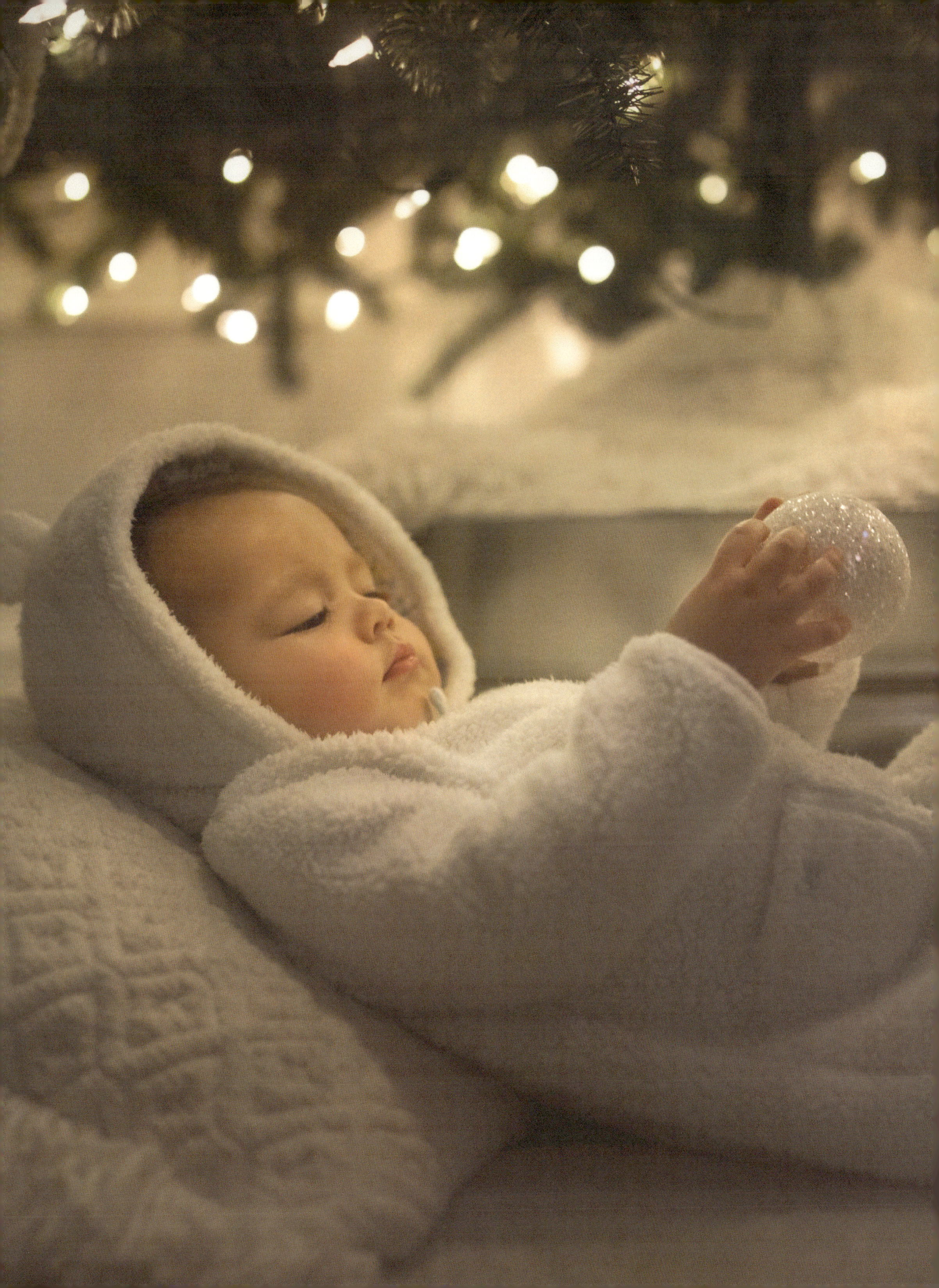

iola ★ JOY

"Be anxious for nothing, but in everything by prayer and supplication with thanksgiving let your requests be made known to God. And the peace of God, which surpasses all comprehension, will guard your hearts and your minds in Christ Jesus."

And ... you might be thinking what happened to my husband? My strong, brave son immediately started CPR, called the paramedics, and saved my husband's life. We got another chance. It changed our lives. It had to. We attempt to get it right. We aren't always successful, but we listen for God's voice and thank Him for His peace in this one gorgeous life.

Become an expert in living in the moment.

Mary Mahan-Deatherage is a freelance writer, brand designer and strategic planner.

MMD Creative is her flagship company specializing in branding and strategic planning for small businesses. She owns *Spoken Women*, a creative community bringing the Catholic perspective to the world through bold writing, podcasts, and art. Her blog, *Divine, Clever, or Whatever* is a Christ-driven endeavor to lighten your soul through her uplifting stories. Mary is a mom of two and Mimi to a pair of rambunctious grandsons. She and her husband, Greg, are enjoying their vibrant, amusing, busy empty-nester life in Dixon, Illinois in the 127-year-old Craftsman home where she grew up. mmd-creative.com, spokenwomen.com, divinecleverorwhatever.com

Dance in the kitchen like no one's watching

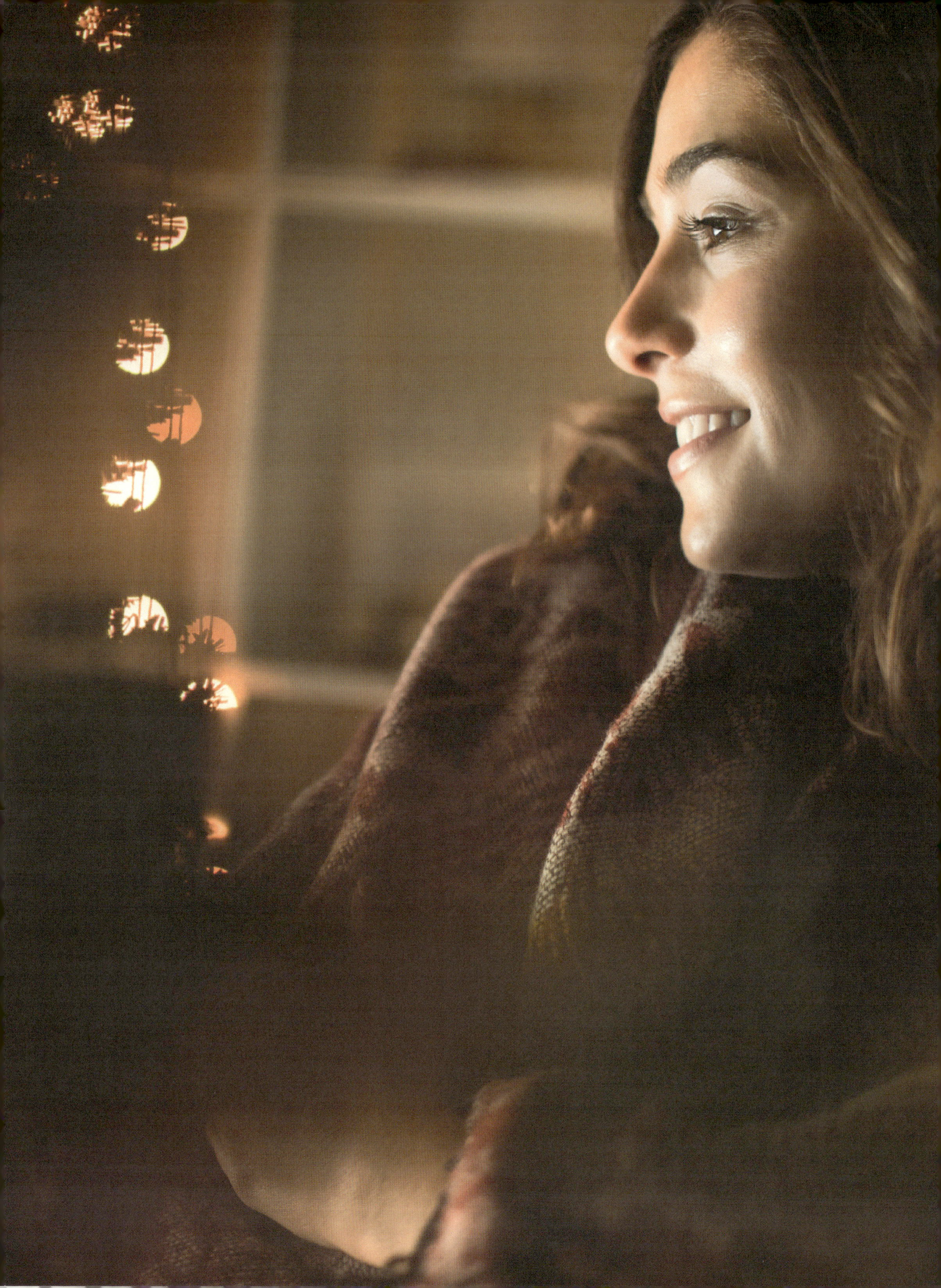

The snow under my feet

Noreen Sevret

The snow gently falls around me as I take a walk on the brick sidewalk in my city, leaving snowy footprints behind for someone else to walk through. I feel the cold air on my cheeks on this evening shortly before Christmas, stopping to look in storefronts with all the pretty things in the windows. Every store on Market Street is decorated for Christmas, and there are twinkling lights in every window I pass. The trees beside the sidewalks are covered with an array of white lights, lighting my way through the darkness of the evening. I find myself feeling quite filled with delight in these quiet moments. I have walked these streets every Christmas for many years now and know just which stores I like to linger longer in front of. I finally reach my favorite store. Whenever I walk in its doors, the beauty on display captivates me. I find nostalgia here, home décor items, homemade chocolates, jewelry, cards, books, and simple pretty things to buy as a gift for that someone special on my gift list. I also like how they wrap the gifts I buy with pretty packaging so they are ready to put under the Christmas tree when I get home!

On my way home, I visit another store up the street that has been here for decades, a local pizza shop where I meet up with my husband for a pizza and soda while the snow continues to fall outside. We enjoy the noise of being in this busy crowded space, yet alone together in a booth where we talk about our moments, our memories, and savor the pepperoni and cheese pizza before us.

With many seasons behind me and my walk a little bit slower than it used to be, on the way out I find my heart filled with memories, making me smile as I feel the warmth of the mittens in my pocket and a reminder of the friend of mine who made them. The longing of these moments have a way of winding their way into my heart to stay for a long time once the snow begins to fall in the winter season!

Even after Christmas is over, I find a walk in the snow to be something that brings me comfort in anticipation of the New Year ahead of me. The lights on Market Street stay lit long after all the presents are unwrapped and the Christmas trees are taken down. They light up the way for snowy evening walks for a long time after the holidays are over.

The longing in my heart that comes with the season of snow falling is reminiscent of years past, going all the way back to my childhood, back to the days of my marriage and young love, the times when my son was little and seeing snow for the first time, walking hand in hand with my husband on cold snowy nights, and times when I felt closer to God in the snowdrift times of my soul. There also comes a longing of sadness and often loneliness that accompanies the snowy season, wishing for "long ago times" and re-visiting times of loss from past winter snows. They both have a place within my heart as the snow collects on the ground outside like the memories have collected in my heart.

On a snowy evening walk in the beginning of the season, I lift my head upwards and see the darkness of the sky and the tiny lights on the nearby trees. I find a tug deep within me longing for much more of the season's warmth and delight than for traveling the path down the lonely road of loss and sadness that can come on dark winter days. What helps me get through lonely times of the soul in winter, when the days are short and I come home from work in the dark, is my intentional list of re"joy"cing. I know, I am spelling it differently. That's intentional to keep me remembering the reasons behind it! I have determined to pile a snowbank inside my heart — built with wonder and rejoicing in the winter season, as I walk with the quietness of snowflakes falling on my face. In reflecting on before, during, and after the holidays, this is how I have found and keep "joy" in the middle of re"joy"cing in the middle of it all:

1. **Remembering good times**
Being intentional in remembering times of gladness helps to embrace ordinary moments.

2. **Realising blessings**
Making a list of things to be thankful for and writing them down on a regular basis helps the heart remain grateful. One year I bought a tiny journal I kept with me throughout the day. It allowed me to add to it when otherwise I may have forgotten to write in it.

3. **Reaching out**
Encouraging others and bringing comfort and cheer to someone else who is hurting helps take the focus off my post-holiday blahs and my own difficulty of getting through the long winter.

4. **Refreshing my heart**
Reading God's Word refreshes and renews the inside of the heart. In return, the Word gives strength to endure and helps thankfulness rise. It helps me walk through seasons where "snowdrifts in life" are deeper than what I think I can walk through. I glance through the Amplified Bible to Romans 15:13, which reads, "May the God of hope fill you with all joy and peace in believing [through the experience of your faith] that by the power of the Holy Spirit you will abound in hope and overflow with confidence in His promises."

5. **Resting in quiet moments**
Learning to rest in quiet moments is much like walking on a quiet evening in the snow. Rest takes ordinary moments and puts a zip of extraordinary in them, falling quiet around me and covering the inside of me. I find a snowy evening synonymous with needed rest on a regular basis, giving me a much needed pause. It fills me up inside, giving me a space I need to dwell in. Rest gives treasured moments in time and a peace that no one can take away.

6. **Restoring my soul**
My soul is restored when I let God lead me beside still and quiet waters [Psalm 23 is my favorite]. Like I restore an old broken piece of furniture, God restores the "old" parts of me that have become broken. He restores me as I walk through ordinary moments. I am restored when I walk in places where I feel His presence and surrender to His leading. Looking for something beautiful in each of my days helps my heart feel restored when I see evidence of God in that place of beauty.

So, when the first snow starts to fall each winter season, I pull out my re"joy"cing list and keep looking at it from time to time. I need it at the beginning of wintertime when the first snow falls and in the middle of the season when wrapping paper from the gifts under the Christmas tree are scattered all over the floor on Christmas Day.

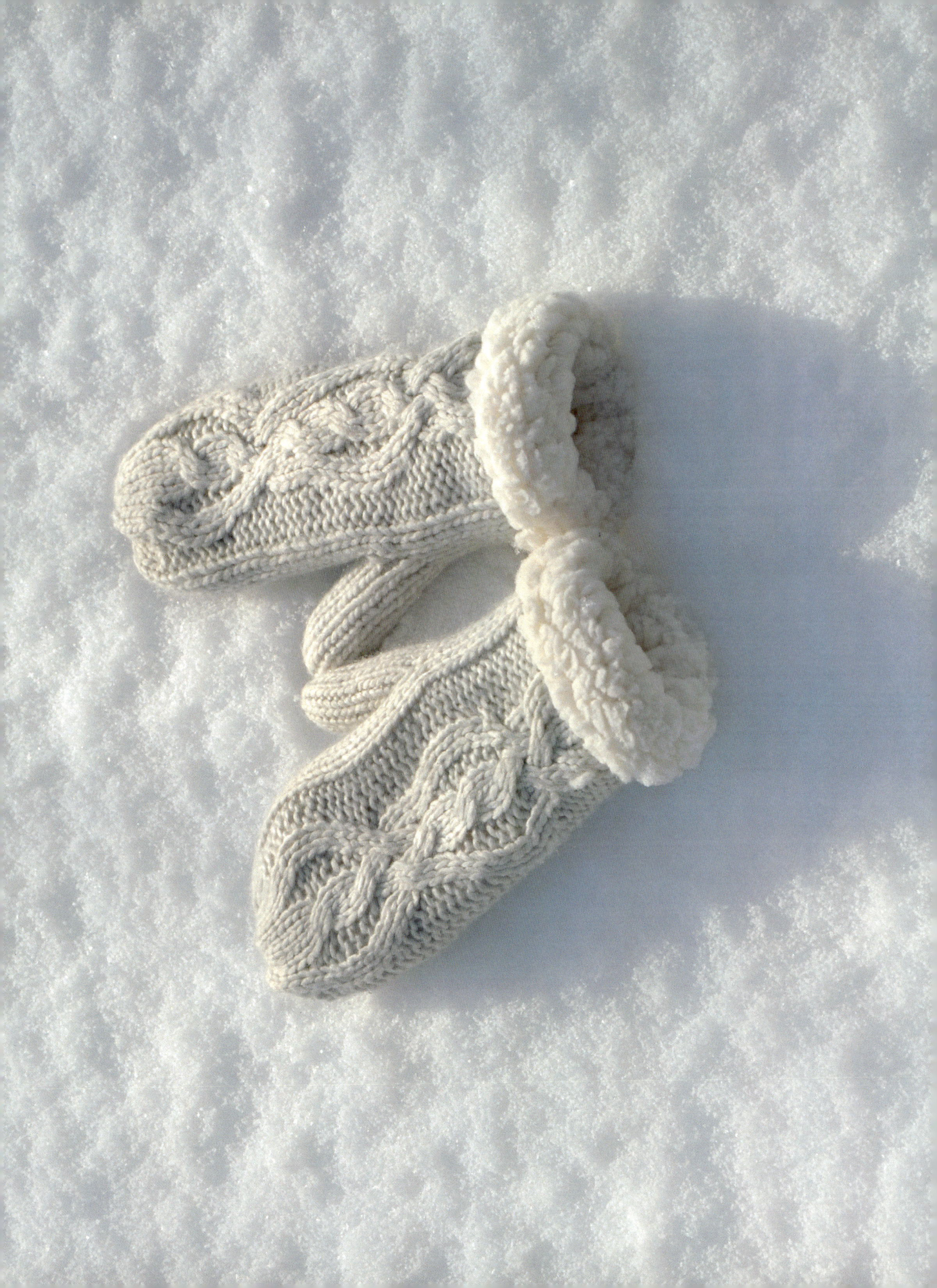

iola * JOY

I need its reminders as the season of snow continues, here in upstate New York, long after the New Year when I really need inspiration and hope for those post-Christmas blues and weariness that often catches hold of me. I surely need it when I wish the snow would simply go away after months and months of it falling everywhere. I find the re"joy"cing list to be something that helps keep my heart wondering of God's goodness and gifts, instead of wandering where my emotions try to pull me.

I find myself sitting on the couch writing tonight, yet again, on another snowy evening. The hot cup of French vanilla cappuccino on the table next to me, topped off with a generous portion of whipped cream, helps me to embrace the ordinary winter evening moments of snow falling and to delight in the beauty of it covering the sidewalk outside my window. I glance at my journal and the words written there from my heart, and find comfort in my view from where I sit, which includes my husband and our son's dog sitting near each other over by the window. Blessings abound in this snowy season called winter as I am tucked away here in this warm place I call home.

Noreen Sevret lives on a pictures-que river in Upstate New York with her husband and their son. She has a passion for finding beauty in unexpected places from behind the lens of her camera and writing about how God speaks to her heart through that picture. She facilitates journaling classes at her church. Noreen enjoys spending time with family, writing worship songs, playing the piano, reading, participating on book launch teams, going out for coffee with friends, and going to beautiful places in NYS and beaches in NJ with her husband. She also works as an office manager for a local funeral home. www.noreensevret.com IG: @writerbytheriver.

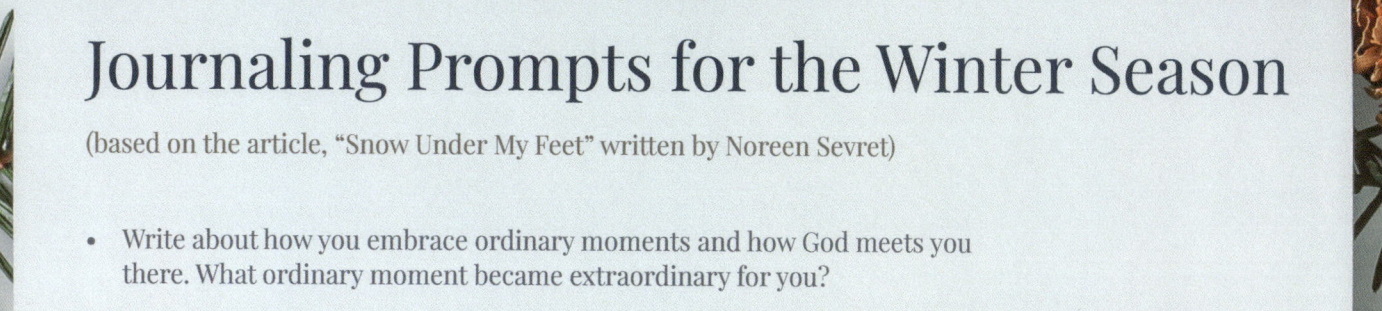

Journaling Prompts for the Winter Season

(based on the article, "Snow Under My Feet" written by Noreen Sevret)

- Write about how you embrace ordinary moments and how God meets you there. What ordinary moment became extraordinary for you?

- Start a list of things to be thankful for. Keep it going in the new year. Share it with your family or a friend. Take it with you throughout the day so you can add to it when thankfulness rises inside.

- Write about a time when you reached out to someone else who was hurting. How did it change you?

- Write about a season when the "snowdrifts in life" were too deep for you to walk in and how you made it through with God's help.

- Write about how you have experienced rest and/or how you yearn to experience rest in your life.

- Write about ways God has restored you. If you are waiting for that restoration, write about what you would like to experience.

- Think about "One Word" you feel God leading you to for the New Year to experience in a new way and to walk in throughout the year. Do a word study on this "One Word" — looking up meanings, synonyms, word origins, etc. Find this "One Word" in the Bible and study the verses it is mentioned in.

- What would you like to change in the New Year? Write your thoughts about it and how it will help you grow personally? Write down a prayer to God about it.

- In your writing, find a scripture verse that goes along with what you are journaling about. If you don't know where to find one, googling "verses about _____" will help you find some options to look up.

- To go deeper, find a group of friends to journal with and share your writings with each other. Gathering around a table with a group of women will break down walls as you each share about your life. You will find that you are not alone.

iola ★ JOY

Stitching Guide

Satin stitch petals
6 strands DMC#927
French knot center
3 strands DMC#3852

Back stitch
3 strands DMC#3051

Back stitch the stem
Leaf stitch the leaves
4 strands DMC#3052

French knots
6 strands DMC#3852

French knots
Vary your sizes by wrapping
1, 2 or 3 times around the needle
6 strands DMC#224

Satin stitch petals
6 strands DMC#3041
French knot center
3 strands DMC#3852

Back stitch the stem
Leaf stitch the leaves
6 strands DMC#3051

Back stitch
6 strands DMC#927

Satin stitch petals
6 strands DMC#3826
French knot center
3 strands DMC#3852

Back stitch
6 strands DMC#3826

Back stitch
6 strands DMC#3041

See Page 54 for traceable pattern.

This embroidery pattern is published with permission. Please do NOT sell items made using this pattern or redistribute in any way. Do not alter this pattern, distribute or claim it as your own. Please DO make this pattern into something lovely, for your friends.

Follow @tinkerellen on Instagram for more, follow tinkinstiches on YouTube for tutorials and tips.

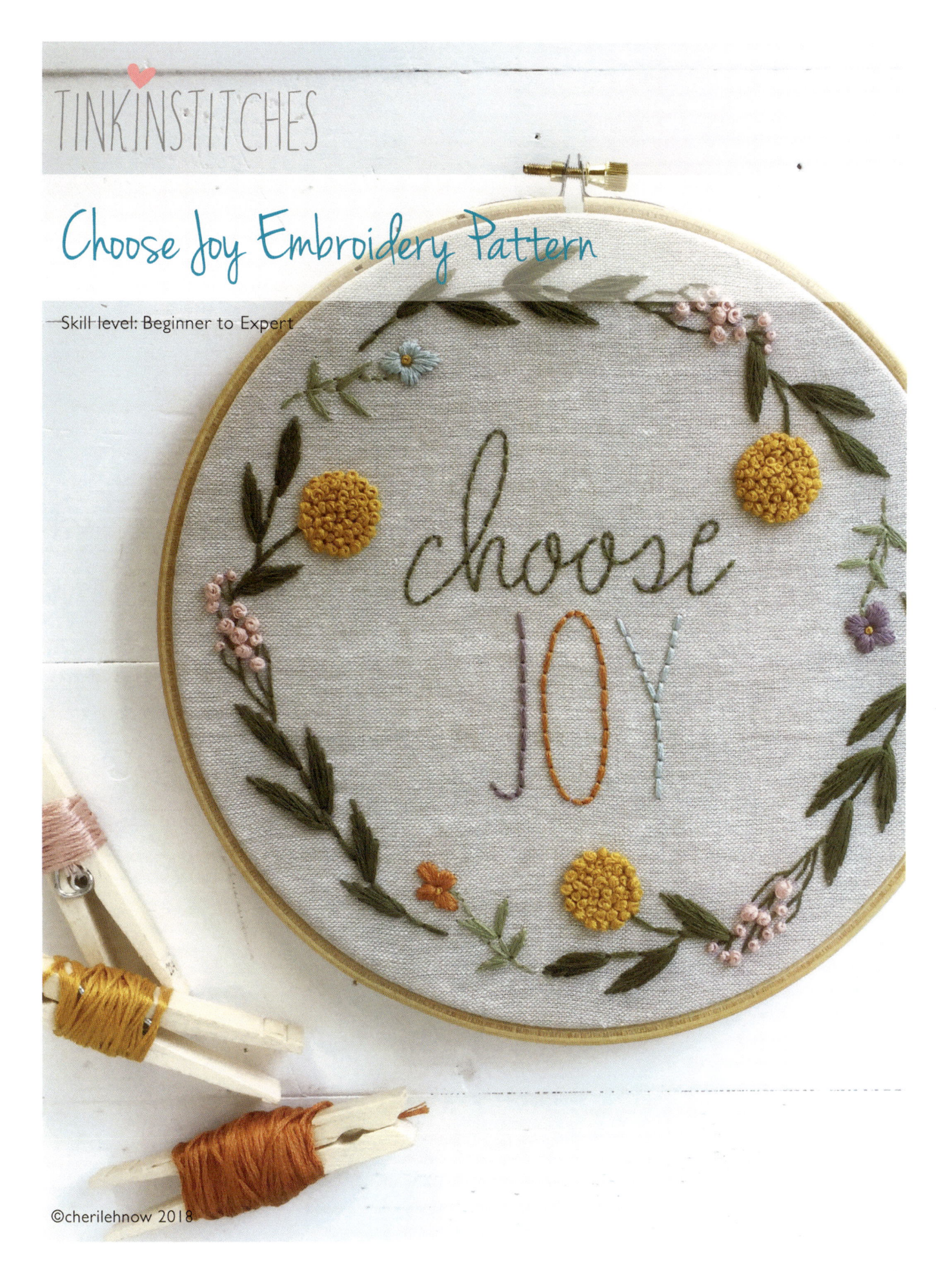

TINKINSTITCHES

Choose Joy Embroidery Pattern

Skill level: Beginner to Expert

©cherilehnow 2018

iola ★ JOY

TINKINSTITCHES
For printing and tracing

choose
JOY

8" hoop

Choose Joy by Cheri Lehnow
This design and pattern is for personal use only.

iola * JOY

Abi writes:

"I had a go at stitching Cheri's pattern, with a slight alteration on colours for a Christmas theme. You can see the finished result and the colours I used above. I love projects that don't take too long to finish, as I loose enthusiasm! This pattern is very easy to follow and didn't take too long to finish."

Satin stitch petals
6 strands DMC#927
French knot center
3 strands DMC#728

Back stitch
3 strands DMC#3051

Back stitch the stem
Leaf stitch the leaves
4 strands DMC#3052

French knots
6 strands DMC#728

French knots
Vary your sizes by wrapping
1, 2 or 3 times around the needle
6 strands DMC#321

Satin stitch petals
6 strands DMC#3041
French knot center
3 strands DMC#728

Back stitch the stem
Leaf stitch the leaves
6 strands DMC#3051

Back stitch
6 strands DMC#927

Satin stitch petals
6 strands DMC#336
French knot center
3 strands DMC#728

Back stitch
6 strands DMC#728

Back stitch
6 strands DMC#3041

55

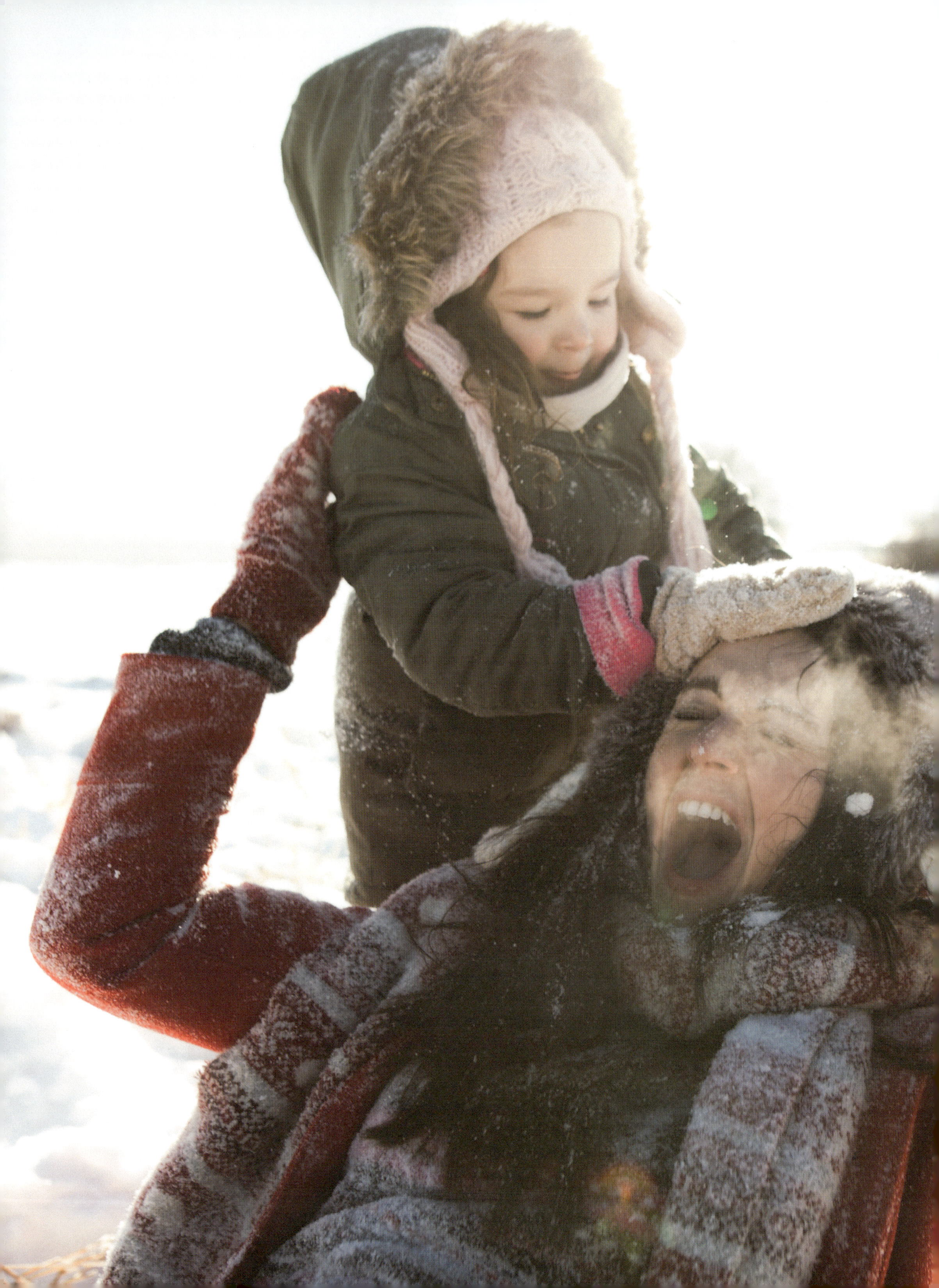

A tool to maximise joy

Mary Mahan Deatherage

Living in the moment is hard. Keeping my mind on the task at hand sometimes takes superpower strength. As a freelancer, I'm often deep in a specific task, for example, writing a lively client article, when suddenly, in mid-sentence, I have an urge to add 'avocados' to my grocery list.

What's up with that?

My go-to prayer at times like these is asking God for concentration while reading and re-reading Colossians 3:23-24

"Whatever you do, do your work heartily, as for the Lord rather than for men, knowing that from the Lord you will receive the reward of the inheritance. It is the Lord Christ whom you serve."

Our work is God's work. Whether you're raising babies or building a bright new career, creating beautiful art, or climbing the corporate ladder, all tasks lead to His glory. But I admit I create reasons to pause during my workday to check out the latest Instagram posts, TikTok fun, or browse my playlists for a new favorite song – all in the name of market research. But when I'm locked in and determined to get a job done, those random mind twinges are a sure way to sidetrack my progress.

If you're like me, you've searched for ways to curb your mental wanderings long enough to accomplish work and home responsibilities. I've found a great solution to ward off those pesky mind pangs. It's *The Pomodoro Technique*. Sounds daunting, I know, but it has worked well for me and might be useful for you too. It's a simple time management practice that helps maximize focus and creative freshness so I can finish that client article or mountain of laundry.

The process is simple and works great for those days when I've put off important tasks – work or personal - and I'm experiencing a bit of overwhelm.

For big work projects, I budget my time into short increments, taking breaks periodically. I work for 25 minutes, then take a five-minute break. During that break I try not to wander to the kitchen for a snack, but hey it's your time – have fun!

Each 25-minute work period is called a 'pomodoro,' named after the Italian word for tomato. Francesco Cirillo, the creator of this method, used a kitchen timer shaped like a tomato as his tool, and Voila! The name stuck.

After four pomodoro work sessions have passed (100 minutes of work time with 15 minutes of short breaks), I then take a longer break of 20-30 minutes. Give yourself a small reward. I take a walk, read a chapter in a fun book or yes, watch one short Netflix episode.

Using your phone, a notebook or calendar page, mark that pomodoro with an 'X.' Note the number of times you had the impulse to procrastinate or switch gears for each 25-minute chunk of time. This helps you recognize your attention length and work to build up your endurance, much like a runner training for a 5k race.

The point is that these frequent breaks keep your mind engaged and the shorter chunks of work time feel more do-able than spending a stretch of endless hours. If you have a large and varied to-do list, using the Pomodoro Technique can help you crank through projects faster by motivating you to adhere

iola * JOY

to specific timing. Spreading a big chore over two or three pomodoro sessions can keep you from getting frustrated and hitting your Netflix app. Minimizing procrastination plus increasing relaxation and fun is a goal for every new year, isn't it?

After trying this method for a week or two you'll be in a great rhythm and will notice your free time is longer and more enjoyable and your stress has diminished.

My goal in the new year is to spend time with the people I love and enjoy my free time without stressing over my undone work tasks (said, me, the procrastinator Queen!). Maybe the Pomodoro Technique is one resolution to maximize your joy in the coming year, too.

The Pomodoro Technique link is www.francescocirillo.com/pages/pomodoro-technique. I'm not in any way associated with this company.

Mary Mahan-Deatherage is a freelance writer, brand designer and strategic planner.

MMD Creative is her flagship company specializing in branding and strategic planning for small businesses. She owns *Spoken Women*, a creative community bringing the Catholic perspective to the world through bold writing, podcasts, and art. Her blog, *Divine, Clever, or Whatever* is a Christ-driven endeavor to lighten your soul through her uplifting stories.

Mary is a mom of two and Mimi to a pair of rambunctious grandsons. She and her husband, Greg, are enjoying their vibrant, amusing, busy empty-nester life in Dixon, Illinois in the 127-year-old Craftsman home where she grew up. mmd-creative.com, spokenwomen.com, divinecleverorwhatever.com

iola ∗ JOY

When they saw the star, they were overwhelmed with joy.

Matthew 2: 10

I don't know what to do!" cried Scrooge, laughing and crying in the same breath; and making a perfect Laocoön of himself with his stockings.

"I am as light as a feather, I am as happy as an angel, I am as merry as a schoolboy. I am as giddy as a drunken man. A merry Christmas to everybody! A happy New Year to all the world."

A Christmas Carol
Charles Dickens

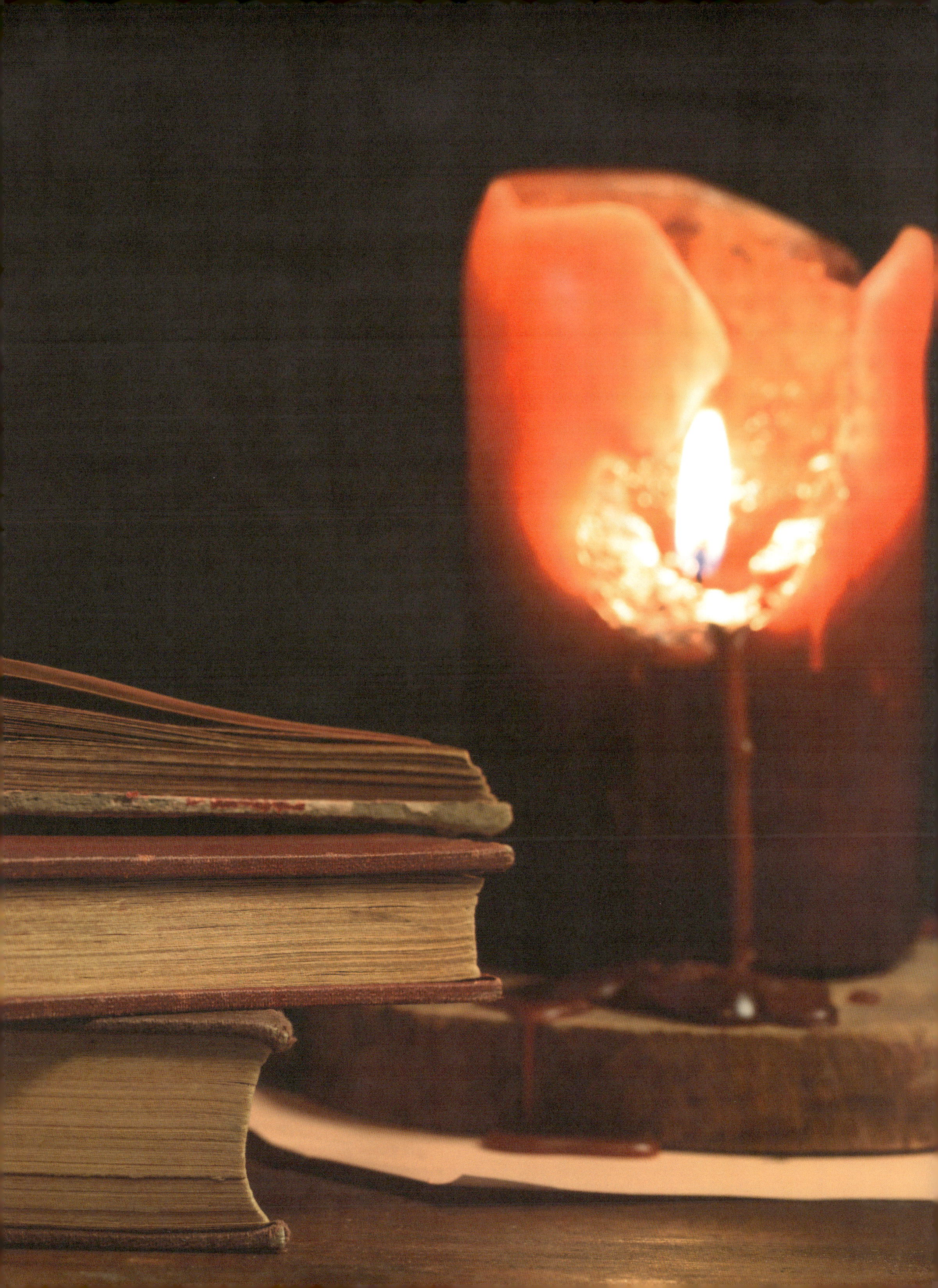

Light as a feather

Abi Partridge

Feathers Wall Hanging

3mm Single Strand Macrame cord
2mm and 3mm macrame cord
Scissors
Pole, stick or twig

1. Cut a piece of cord that is around 92 cm long. This piece of cord will run down the middle of your quill. Fold in half and tie a knot at the top. Leaving a long loop at the top to tie around the wood.

2. Cut pieces of cord – around 43 cm long. Fold in two, place loop under spine and thread ends over the spine and through it's own loop. This is a Cow Hitch tie. A Cow Hitch tie is the opposite of the Lark's Head Knot. If you somehow happened to make a Lark's Head bunch and afterward flip your work over you would see a Cow Hitch tie.

3. Tie one piece on the left, one piece on the right, etc. Repeat until you have about 6 cm of cord left.

4. With the two spine lengths tie a twofold bunch at the lower part of your work.

5. Brush out your string.

6. Using a template or freehand if you are brave, cut a feather shape aroud the edges of your work.

7. Make more feathers and loop over a branch or driftwood.

8. Tie a length of cord at each end of the wood to hang it from.

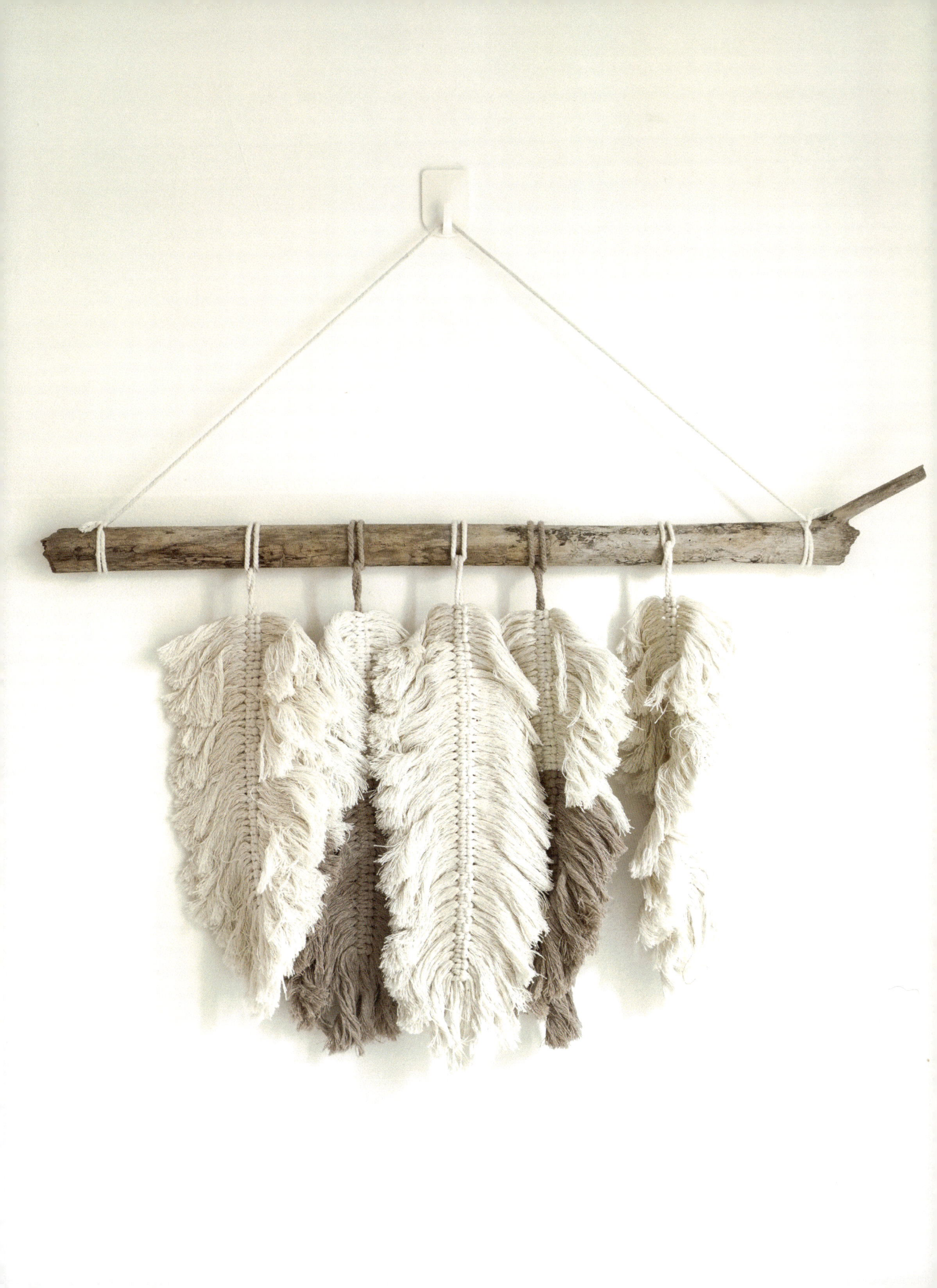

Joy playlist

God Rest Ye Merry Gentlemen – Pentatonix
I need a little silent night – Amy Grant
Joy of the Lord – Maverick City Music
Joy to the World – The Oxford Trinity Choir
Joyful, Joyful, Lord we adore thee – Maverick City Music
Bells – Audrey Assad
God is good – Francesa Battistelli
Star of wonder (Gloria) – (feat. Dear Gravity) Salt of the Sound

SCAN ME

My soul will be
joyful in the Lord

Psalms 35: 9

I have told you
this so that my joy
may be in you and
that your joy may be
complete.

John 15:11

Even though
you do not see
him now, you believe
in him and are filled
with an inexpressible
and glorious joy

1 Peter 1: 8-9

May the God of
hope fill you with
all joy and peace in
believing, so that by the
power of the Holy Spirit
you may abound
in hope

Romans 15: 13

The joy of the Lord
is your strength

Nehemiah 8: 10

The Lord has
done great things
for us, and we are
filled with joy.

Psalm 126: 3

Be joyful
in hope, patient
in affliction,
faithful in prayer

Romans 12: 12

The prospect
of the
righteous is joy.

Proverbs 10: 28

Consider it pure
joy my brothers
and sisters whenever
you face trials of
many kinds

James 1: 2

Verses of Joy

winter

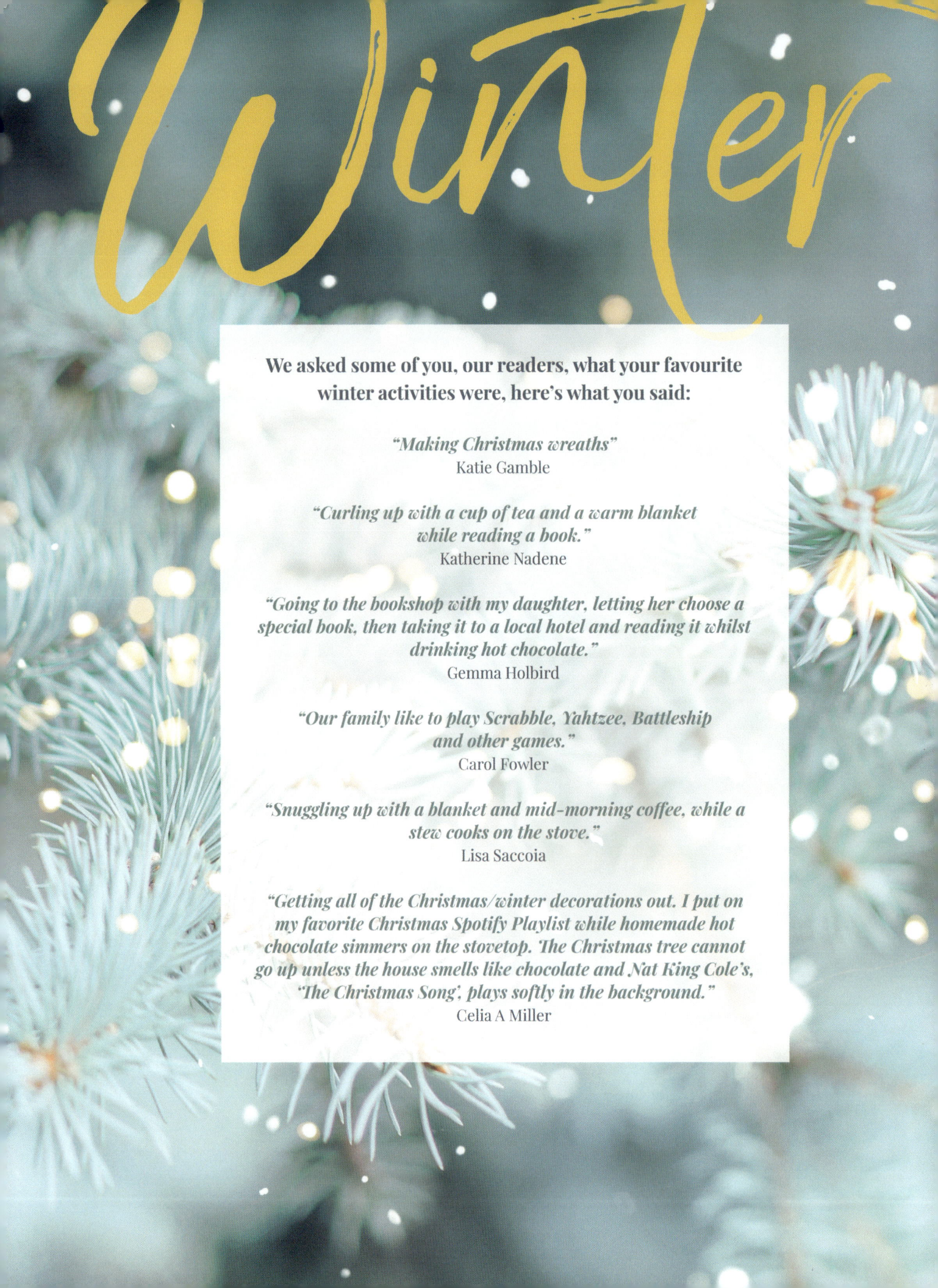

We asked some of you, our readers, what your favourite winter activities were, here's what you said:

"Making Christmas wreaths"
Katie Gamble

"Curling up with a cup of tea and a warm blanket while reading a book."
Katherine Nadene

"Going to the bookshop with my daughter, letting her choose a special book, then taking it to a local hotel and reading it whilst drinking hot chocolate."
Gemma Holbird

"Our family like to play Scrabble, Yahtzee, Battleship and other games."
Carol Fowler

"Snuggling up with a blanket and mid-morning coffee, while a stew cooks on the stove."
Lisa Saccoia

"Getting all of the Christmas/winter decorations out. I put on my favorite Christmas Spotify Playlist while homemade hot chocolate simmers on the stovetop. The Christmas tree cannot go up unless the house smells like chocolate and Nat King Cole's, 'The Christmas Song', plays softly in the background."
Celia A Miller

Joys

"Reading an inspirational book and reflecting on it while sitting next to our stone fireplace with a crackling warm fire and a cup of coffee."
Laura Rizkallah

"Gathering with friends around the fire pit to share a meal (usually chili or chowder) and good red wine. It's even better when it's snowing!"
Michelle Layer Rahal

"In the winter I take a twenty minute walk in the woods daily. I drink hot tea before bed. I warm the bed with a heating pad before getting under the covers. I love that it gets dark early!"
Edgy

"My absolute favorite activity in the cozier months is hand embroidery by a fire."
Cynthia Stuckey

"My favourite activity during winter is crocheting something like a rug or a scarf to keep my loved ones warm. Even better with the wood fire going and a spicy chai latte on oat milk while crocheting!"
Sherri Smith

"My favorite is snowshoeing! (Canada life!)"
Laura Thomas

*The desert and the parched land will be glad; the wilderness will rejoice and blossom.
Like the crocus, it will burst into bloom; it will rejoice greatly and shout for joy.*
Isaiah 35: 1–2

Get the party started

Conversation starters for a New Years Eve party. Cut out, place in a bowl, pass around and take one to answer.

Hardest you laughed this year was when...	**Favourite song this year.**	**Best piece of advice you were given this year.**
Best book you read this year.	**Best moment of the year.**	**Favourite item of the year.**
Best conversation you had this year.	**Best news of the year.**	**Most overrated story this year.**
Biggest lesson learnt this year.	**Best thing you did for someone else this year.**	**Best movie this year.**

Book introductions

Joyful
The surprising power of ordinary things to create extraordinary happiness

Ingrid Fetell Lee
Rider / 2018 / ISBN: 978-1846045400

Ingrid Fetell Lee is a designer and in this book explores how making small changes to your surroundings can create extraordinary happiness in your life. You might think from the title that it is a superficial look at luxury goods or an ode to consumerism but it is not. Drawing from neuroscience and psychological insights, she reveals how the seemingly mundane spaces and objects we interact with every day have surprising effects on our mood.

If you are looking for the reasons why and how to create more joy in your life, this part story, intelligent look at the power of small changes you can make to your environment will help you live a healthier and more joyful life.

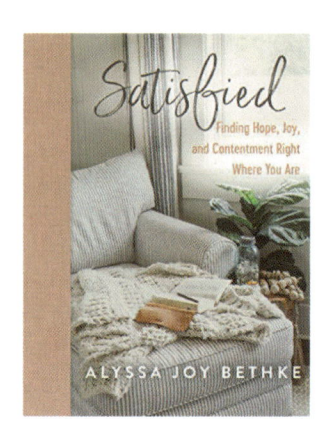

Satisfied
Finding hope, joy and contentment right where you are

Alyssa Bethke
Worthy Books / June 2021 / ASIN: B08HHZTGJV

Story-led essays combined with beautiful home images and recipes, this book will help you cultivate and embrace beauty in your life.

With all of its expectations and contradictions, this world can take a toll on us. Be skinny, but not too skinny. Work and hustle but stay home and be a good mum. Be wild and free while tidy and pure. Love your husband but be independent.

Alyssa walks you through issues that rob you of joy and helps you recognize them for what they are: distractions. touching on topics like fear, worry, dissatisfaction, anxiety, and body image. The book will show you all the ways you are enough and not alone in your fight to have a fulfilling life.

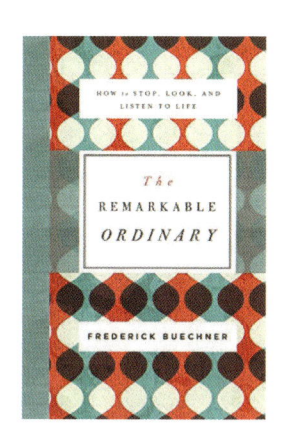

The Remarkable Ordinary
How to stop, look and listen to life
Fredrick Buechner

Zondervan / November 2017 / ASIN: B06XFM3YBP

A classic book to help you learn to see God's remarkable works in the everyday ordinary of your life.

Your life may seem predictable and your work insignificant until you look at your life as Frederick Buechner does.

Frederick Buechner reveals how to stop, look, and listen to your life. He reflects on how both art and faith teach us how to pay attention to the remarkableness right in front of us, to watch for the greatness in the ordinary, and to use our imaginations to see the greatness in others and love them well.

Listen to the call of a bird or the rush of the wind, to the people who flow in and out of your life. The ordinary points you to the extraordinary God who created and loves all of creation, including you. Pay attention to these things as if your life depends upon it. Because, of course, it does.

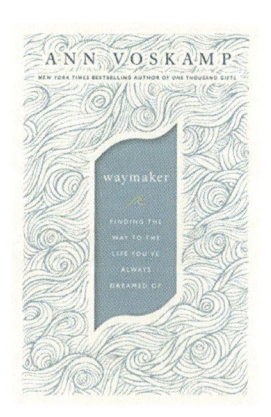

Waymaker
Finding the way to the life you've always dreamed of
Ann Voskamp

Thomas Nelson / Mar 2022 / ASIN: B08ZMBSR63

It is true: heartache, grief, suffering, obstacles, they all come in waves. There is no controlling life's storms; there is only learning the way to walk through the waves. In WayMaker, Ann Voskamp hands us a map that makes meaning of life, that shows the way through to the places we've only dreamed of reaching, by a way we never expected. Voskamp reveals how God is present in the totality of our lives, making a way for the marriage that seems impossible, for the woman who longs for a child of her own, for the parents who ache for the return of their prodigal, for the sojourner caught between a rock and a hard place, and for the wayfarer who feels as though there is no way through to her dreams.

We can encounter the WayMaker in surprising ways and begin to see Him not only making poetry out of pain but working in every miraculous detail of our lives. Even now, the Way is making the way to walk through waves and into a life more deeply fulfilling than our wildest dreams.

But the angel said to them,
"Don't be afraid, for look,
I proclaim to you
good news of great joy
that will be for all the people:
Today in the city of David
a savior was born for you,
who is the Messiah, the Lord."

Bookmarks

Cut out and keep

Joy: the smell of a new book & fresh coffee

Glad tidings of great joy

Joy to the world, the Lord has come

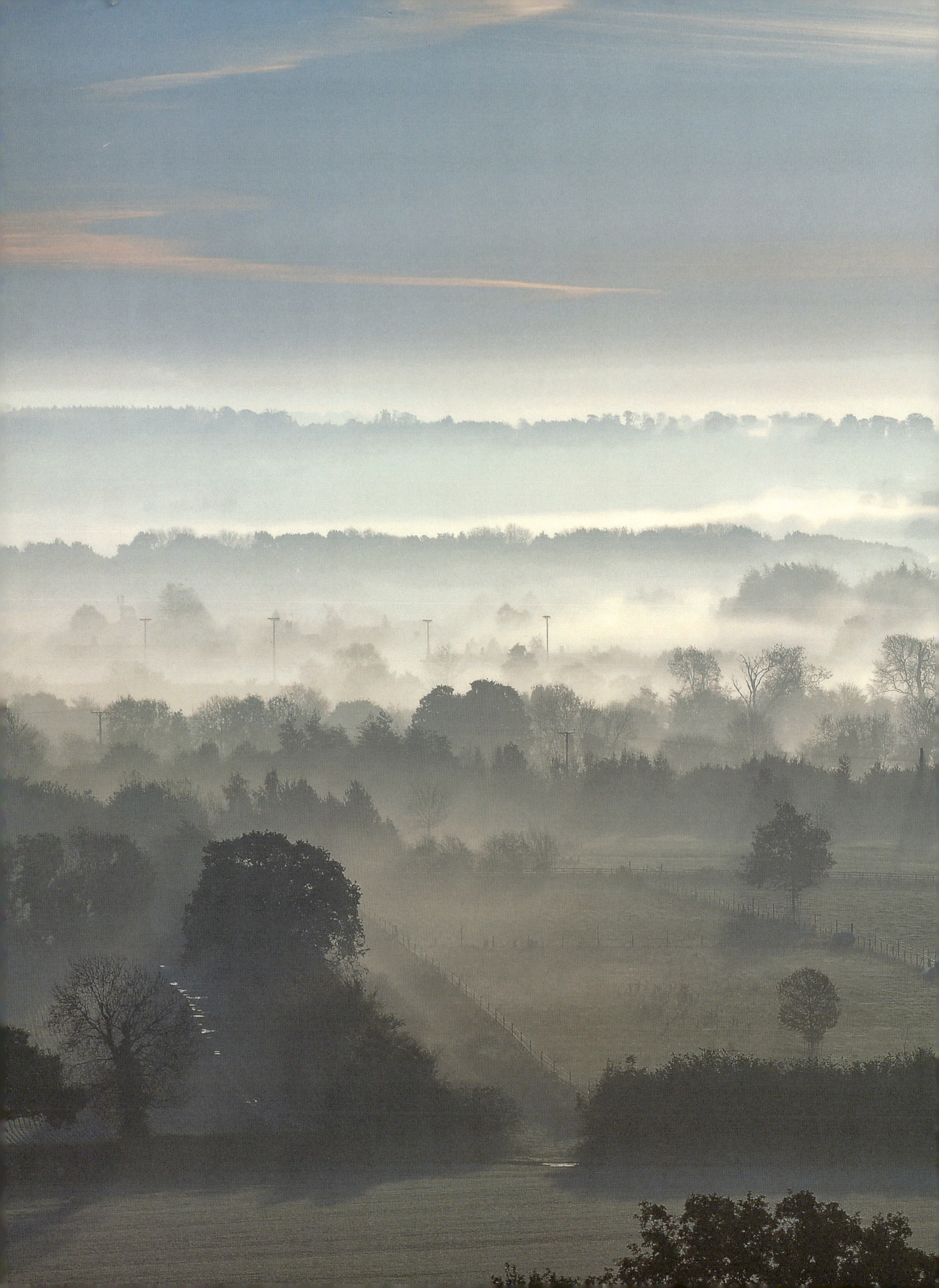

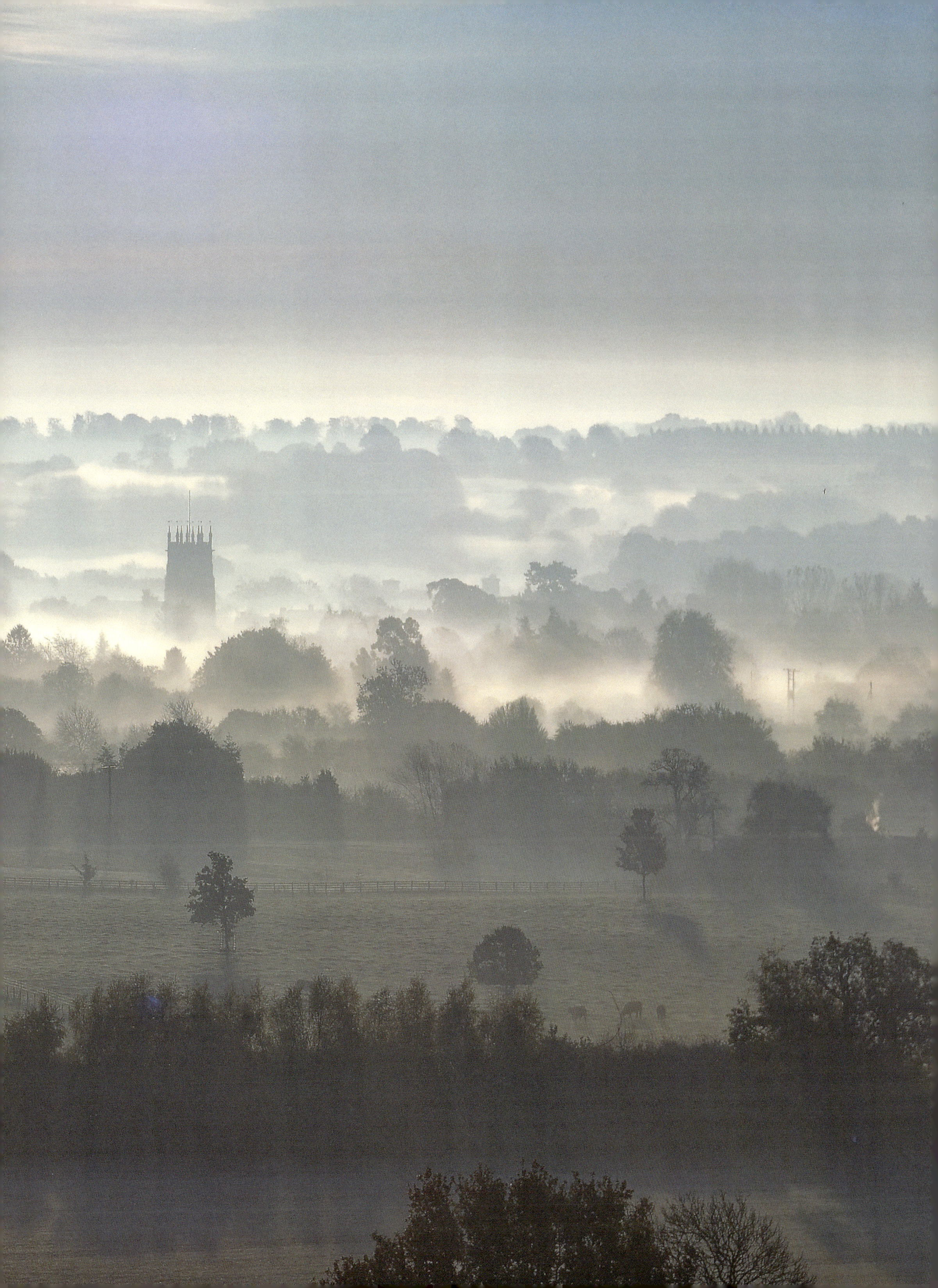

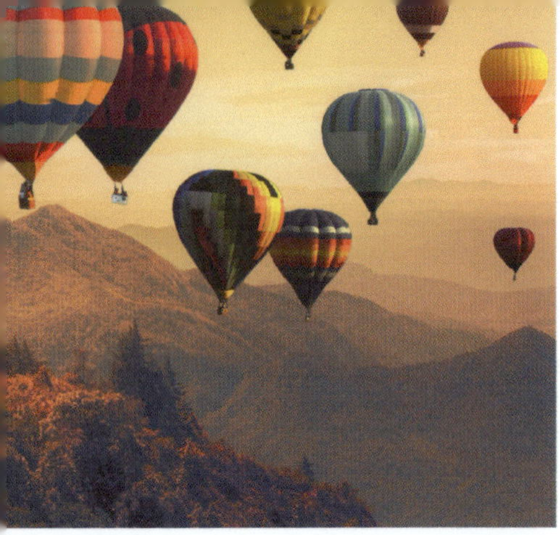
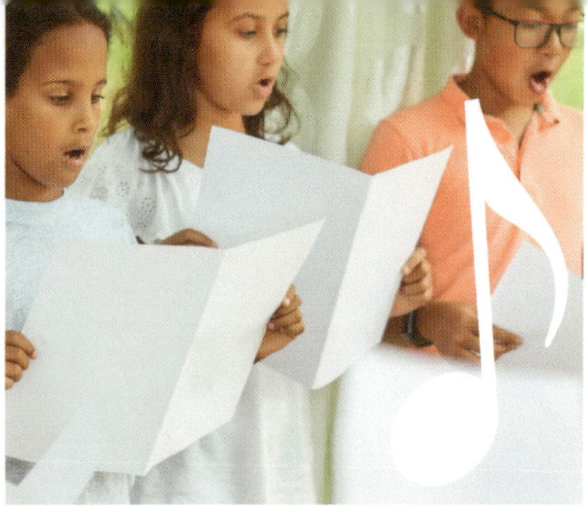
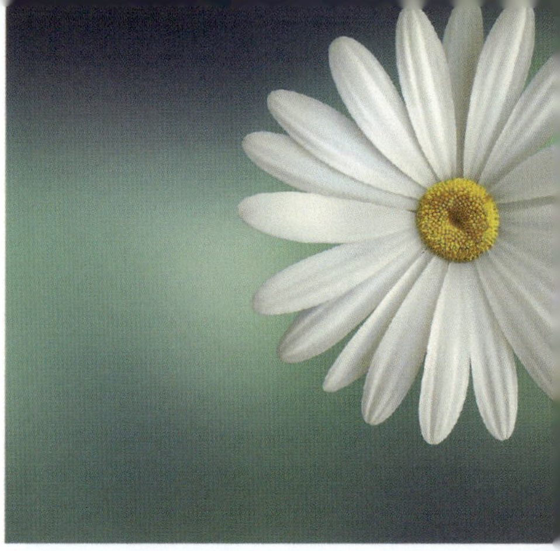
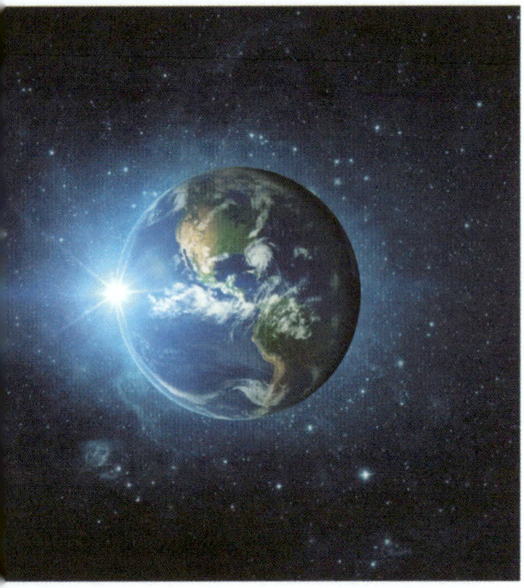
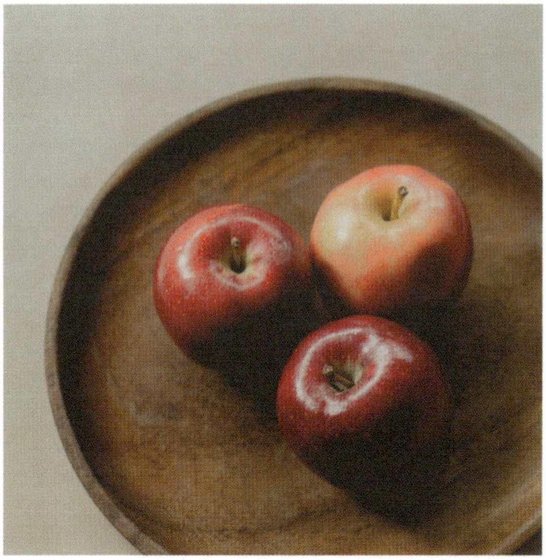
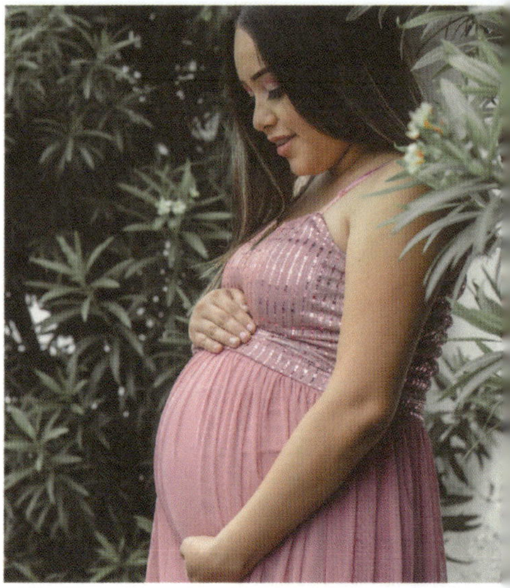
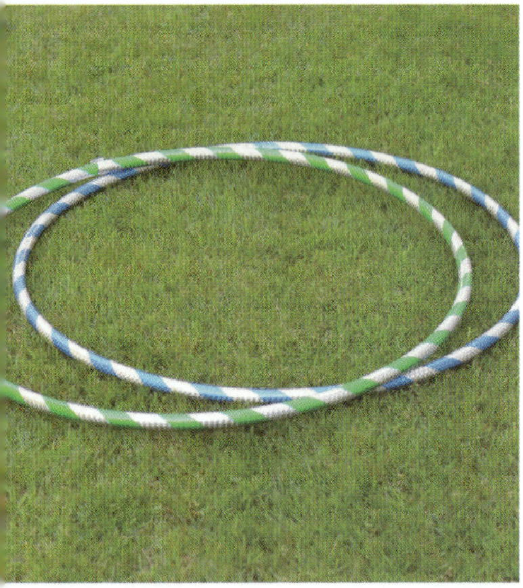
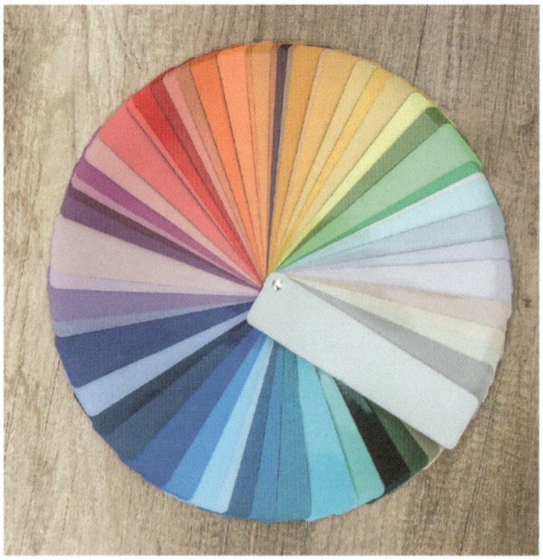
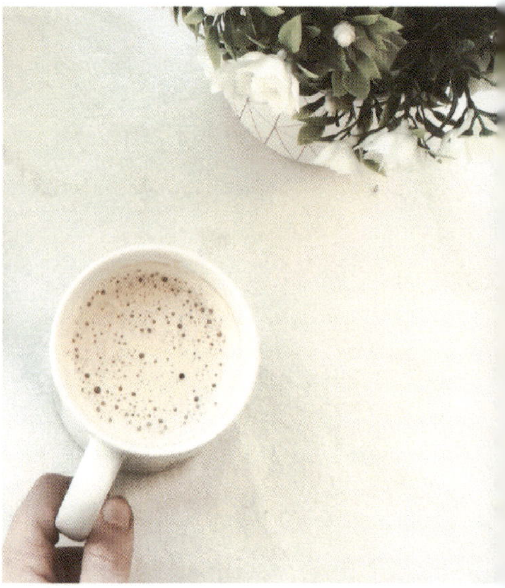
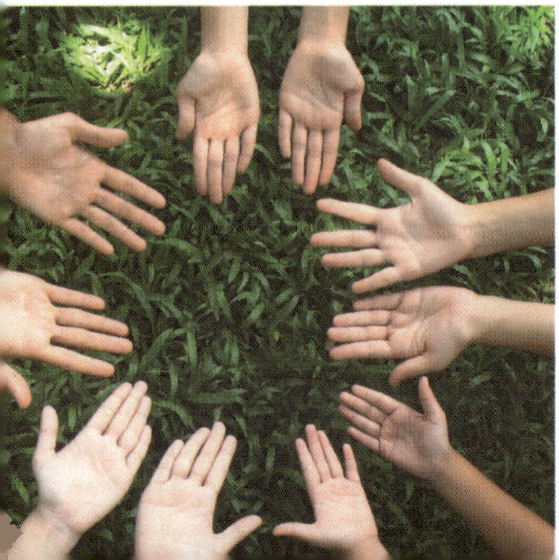
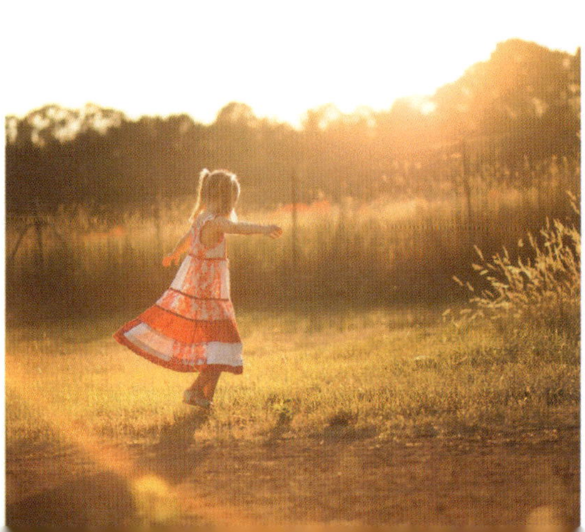
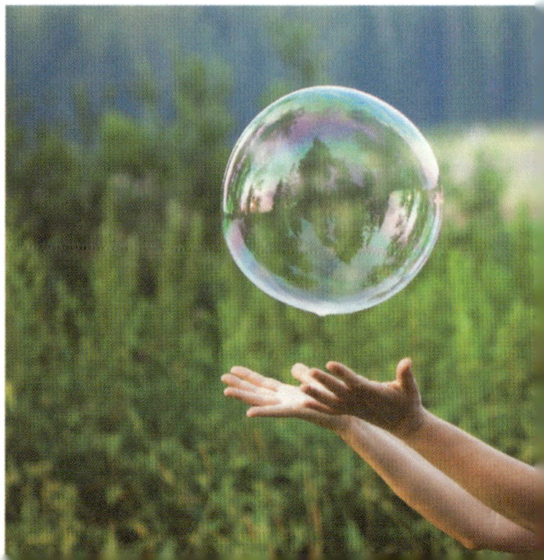

The shape of joy

Abi Louise

"If I ask you to name a joyful shape, what's the first one that comes to mind? For many people I've asked over the years the answer is a circle." Joyful - Ingrid Fetell Lee

This comes as no surprise when I think of all the shapes of joyful things, balloons, confetti, a cup of coffee, plates of delicious food, bubbles catching the light and gently floating up like a dream, the spinning of a pastel striped hula hoop, the soft curl on a newborn's head. A spinning top, a penny flipped to spin on it's edge, the spin of a waltzer at the fairground. The symmetry of a circle is so complete, satisfying somehow in it's completeness. Is it this completeness that resembles joy to us?

Or is a circle the shape of joy because it is the shape of home; our planet, a pregnant tummy, a face, a hug? Can we combine the two? Completeness is a feeling of being home?

A circle is a curved shape, in design curves are associated with femininity and softness. Joy represented in shapes could be described as childish, youthful, feminine and complete.

"The circle's unbroken perimeter and even rate of curvature make it the most stable, complete and inclusive shape. A love of symmetry is one of the best studied human aesthetic preferences. One reason we love symmetry may be that it is an outward symbol of inner harmony". Joyful - Ingrid Fetell Lee

Beyond the physical

What about musical notes, curved balls of sound hung on telephone wires of five and the wide open mouths of a choir, these physical circles of joy create feelings of joy: *"Sing in a group and you experience a rush of hormones associated with mood elevation and reducing symptoms of depression including endorphins and dopamine."* Do Sing: Reclaim your Voice. Find your singing tribe - James Sills. Those round notes of melody in turn inspire dance; the movement of joy. Dancing also releases endorphins and helps you to connect with your inner child and express yourself. Dancing comes in forms of spins and twirls, circular steps and sets. Is the activity of singing and dancing why we associate circles with joy?

How about those metaphorical circles, a friendship circle, the idea of what goes around comes around, the moral arc of justice, renewal, recycling, restoration, - how do these circles play into our idea of joy? A circle is inclusive, it faces all, includes all, it has no sharp edges to cause pain or entrapment. Is joy found in justice, inclusion and comfort?

From this consideration of the shape of the circle; the shape of joy, can we then infer that joy is youthful, complete, feminine, musical, movement, justice, and inclusive?

Is it too much to consider The Creator infused the shape of a circle with joy? That he meant it that way, that circles are meant to show us that joy is found in these things and finding these things actually brings joy? I'd like to think so.

Abi Louise helps entrepreneurs overcome design issues so they can increase income. She lives on the edge of the bookish city of Oxford and the beautiful countryside of the Cotswolds with her three children. www.abilouise.co

Celebrate!

Decoration of Joy

Make your own decoration of joy with the paper circles opposite. Cut out and sew or string together. Cut a slot from the outside to the centre and slot too together for a 3d circle string.

Happy New Year!

iola * JOY

iola ★ JOY

Plan with Purpose & Journal with Joy

Is this true for you?

You love to write down your plan for the week and to celebrate the season, but you feel a little overwhelmed by the blank page. You used to write out your prayers but somehow the time disappeared and you miss pouring out your heart in the same way. You've got a diary for dates and a notebook for notes, but you want to plan your days more intentionally and journal your moments.

Studies have shown that writing is a practice that is good for your wellbeing. Gratitude is a way to chase beauty in life, that in turn increases the amount of beauty you see. The act of writing with a pen on paper is proven to increase our memory of those things and relieves the mind as your hand writes it out.

That's why we created the iola planner & journal.

It's a way to plan and notice your season, month, week, and days beside your daily gratitude & prayers, whilst noting what you are learning & creating.

Gratitude & prayer bring us close to Jesus. We see how our learning and creativity is blooming and blessing others.

Now's the time to start the new year with purpose and joy. Get yours at abipartridge.co.uk/iola-planner-journal

81

Christmas Jewels

Moment to remember

Feast for the eyes

Gifts given & received

Taste of goodness

Scent of the season

Touch of joy

Where I found Jesus

Where I found myself

New Year Joys

Moment to make

Feast for the soul to find

Gifts to give

Goodness to taste

Scents to smell

Joy to sense

Practises to make

Jewels to find

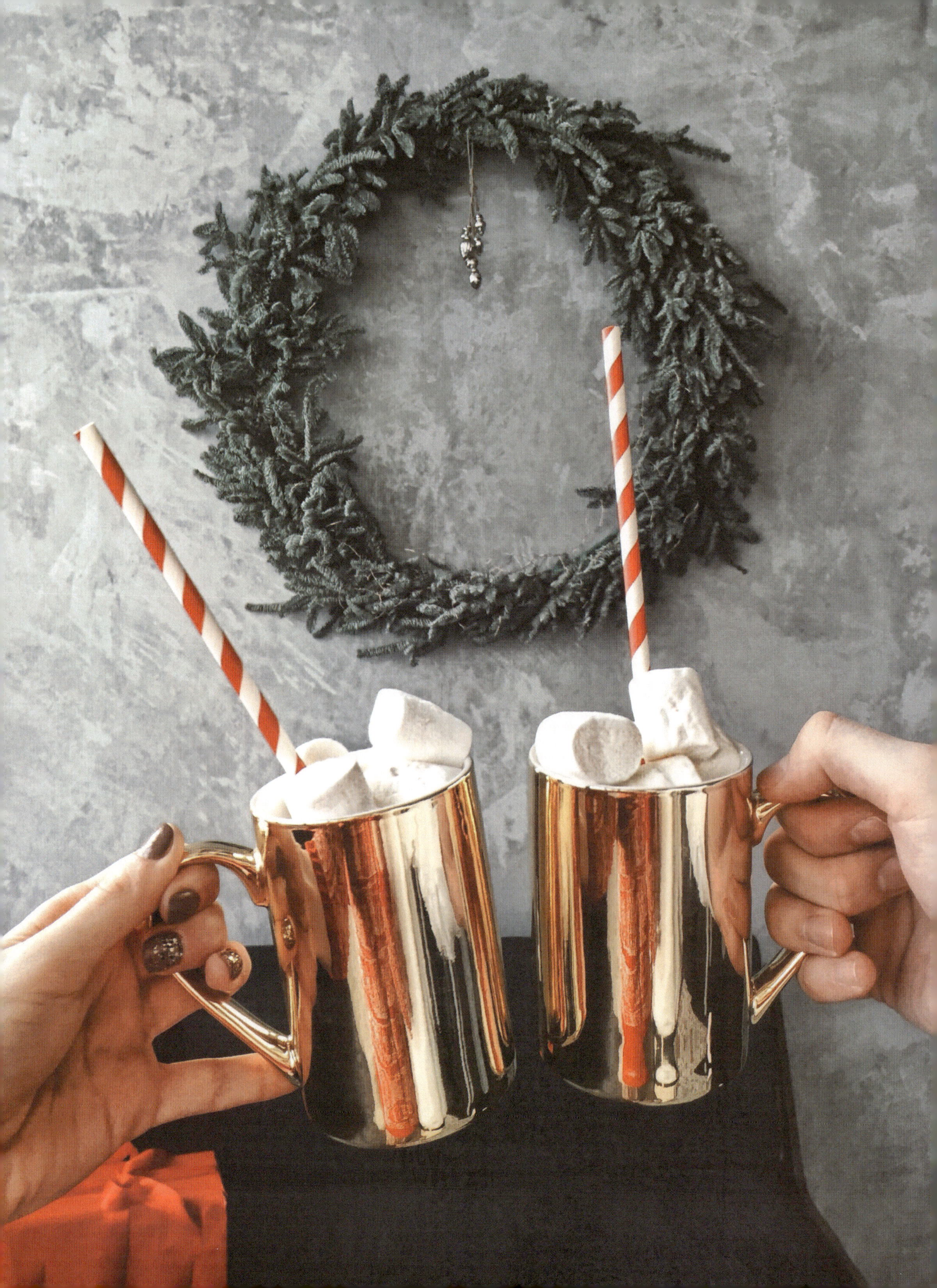

Unexpected Joy

Laura Rizkallah

Once upon a time, in a village far, far, away lived eleven children huddled together waiting for hope to find them.

In another city far, far, away from that African village, lived a woman in an American city looking for something more. She was looking for joy. I was that woman.

In many stories we read of two strangers' lives intersecting through magical encounters of collision in a coffee shop or an airport. Somehow "love" is born. These random intersections alter destinies of each person, and their lives are forever changed. And this all happens because of a random force (maybe a fairy godmother, twitterpated emotions or Cupid) orchestrating the epic encounter in the unforeseen event that has now eternally entwined them. We cheer. We wipe away tears of joy. But is that really joy?

This story of a woman and eleven children isn't about magic or mystical encounters but miracles. This story isn't about random chance meetings, but God appointed times. This story is about how our sovereign and incredible God weaves ordinary, unpredictable endings together and connects them to joy despite the seemingly unknown, ordinary, or long paths of life we often walk. This story is about how joy can be found in the darkest of places, tiniest, forgotten spaces, and in the eyes of tiny, little faces.

Years ago, I was honored to be able to travel to West Africa on a mission trip. While there, we were asked to take food into a local village. We had heard there were some children in need there.

Our driver got directions to the remote location. We stopped and bought rice, water, crackers, and basic hygiene supplies. We drove through vibrant, green forests, through thriving villages, where the smoky scent of fish and banana chips being fried over open fires followed the van we traveled in. I was in love with this country and its people. I felt honored to see such beauty in the landscape and robust lifestyle. We continued over dirt roads, past goats, chickens, and all the beautiful smiles and friendly faces of people watching our large, white, multipurpose, fifteen passenger van traveling over roads that would have been better suited for a safari jeep.

Eventually, we exited busy village life and entered uninhabited, tropical jungles. The roads began to narrow and then turned into wide-ish paths. There were less people and a whole lot more potholes. Every now and again we would pass a woman carrying her children on her back, eggs and fish for sale in a tin basin balanced perfectly on her head and pushing a cart with fruits for sale. I marveled at her strength and grit. We would wave and ask for directions to 'the village' we were looking for. We began to wonder if perhaps this village was more of a hidden city or an unknown people group. The women on the side of the road would smile, nod and wave us forward. Into the jungle deeper and deeper we went.

Finally, we began to smell a scent that indicated we had found another village. That same smokey smell of life being lived over an open fire started to fill our van again. We were close. As soon as the rumble of our jungle-challenged van was heard by the village children, they started running out of the beautiful green foliage all around us. It was a scene out of my wildest dreams. The children cheered and clapped, chased us and waved us into their village. Thankfully, they were as happy to see us as we were to see them.

As we began to interact, laugh, and develop a relationship with these beautiful people, we became aware of a few children that weren't joining the fun. Beyond the small group of people gathering around our poppin' party, we could see a crumbling concrete structure. It was an old, abandoned school with a few rooms. We approached the structure we saw little faces peeking out from behind pillars and old wooden school desks. We had found the children in need.

We entered this school building they had been living in, we came across something I never expected. There, in the dim light filtering through a torn and pieced together curtain waving in the breeze, a small figure appeared to be laying in the shadows on the floor. It was the smallest of these children. He was fevering and unresponsive. He was suffering from malaria, and the villagers and his young friends had tried to find help, but it was too far and too costly. This small boy's condition had become an extreme situation quickly.

We asked many questions and sought many answers in the days to come. These children had been foraging for themselves and taking care of one another. Brought together by stories too long to tell here, they had formed a community of eleven children ranging from the ages of 17 to 2 years old. They were a band of non-related survivors of circumstances over which they had no control. They had survived stories most of us couldn't listen to let alone live through.

These children had found shelter. They each had found each other. And now, we had found them.

We left that village the way we came in, but with nine more seats filled. That van was the perfect vehicle for our mission now!

The next week was spent working with the local government, orphanages, police offices, and village hospitals to help these children in need. It involved so many potty breaks and food stops that I lost track.

Searching for conversation starters throughout the next week, we asked the children if they had ever been to the beach. Afterall, we were in West Africa. The Atlantic Ocean was part of their great land and culture. The children had very little understanding as to what we were talking about. They had heard of the ocean or seen a picture of it here or there, but none of them had been to it. They had not danced in the surf, or been chased by waves, or buried their toes in the sand. As we traveled through days of official paperwork, offices, and officials, we would describe the ocean and tell stories about it to pass the hours of waiting and hoping for help and homes for all of these children. Our promise to them, after securing them in safe homes with the help of local authorities, was to get permission to take them to the ocean. We promised to let them jump, play, and run on the beach.

It was a long week of perseverance and determination by our mission team, but compassion and safety were found for each of these children. The young boy who had malaria was running around and full of life once again. It was time to keep our promise. We loaded up that van with a picnic lunch

Nicole McKibbin nbmcreative.com

iola * JOY

with nine, eager and ocean-ready kids. I heard the ocean waves and the seagulls. I was aware of the heat and the beating sun. I was expecting a great afternoon. What I didn't expect was what I would feel when nine children who had never seen the ocean, never observed the magnificent size, felt the force of the waves, or the warmth of the beach that stretched farther than they had ever been able to see.

The waves crashed all around them and joy crashed over me. Unspeakable, unexpected joy!

I wept as they leapt. Then I laughed. I laughed so hard I felt like I could fly. I couldn't help but jump and play. Their joy had become my joy. The joy of loving them and knowing them and seeing them find a new beginning was more than my heart could handle. I held their little hands. They held my fragile heart. I knew I would never be the same. Their story had become part of mine.

Finding Joy within us

Two thousand years ago there was another child born in a village far-far away called Bethlehem. Not many knew he would appear in a broken down left-for-the-animals-only shed on a starry and ordinary night. He was wrapped in rags. He appeared to be small and insignificant born to two ordinary individuals.

Jesus entered our world in what seemed to be a crazy unexpected way to save our broken, lonely, dark world.

Everything about his arrival appeared ordinary. Obscure. In fact, his birth appeared so ordinary many of us might have missed it. He came to make sure none of us were ever orphaned or alone. Ever. He went to extremes to get to us. He refused to give up his mission. He came to make sure none of us were ever going to have to be abandoned or enslaved to the bondage of sin, shame or suffering. He came to deliver us... and set us free. Not a small birth plan, huh?

Jesus's purpose was greater than anything most people could see or imagine. His life was full of purpose. He healed the blind. Set captives free. Performed miracles. However, His ultimate purpose on this earth wasn't his birth. It was His death. He knew he was born to die.

....for the joy set before Him he endured the cross. Hebrews 12:2 (NIV)

Jesus focused on "the joy" that was set before Him? Is joy really enough to help us endure all things? The birth of my second child felt like it was never going to end. My labor was long. The pain was relentless. As I endured the long hours of what felt like torture, my husband would keep leaning in and whispering a truth that had been apparent to me 9 months prior to this moment but had lost it's power in the middle of my pain. "Honey, the pain is going to be worth the reward." he would tenderly remind me. My son was born, despite my doubt that I would ever survive that kind of intense labor. He was worth it.

My husband knew the secret place inside a runner looking to finish his race or the internal secret of an author who is lost in words but knows the end result of her work is in sight. The joy we find in life is knowing the end result is worth the temporary struggle.

Joy is not what is going on around us but rather what is going on inside of us.

Joy surprises us. It meets us in labor and delivery rooms, dark hallways, lonely schools, the cancer ward, or at a beach in a land that is not your own where you thought you were helping someone else, but instead you find out they were helping you! We must remember the joy in us and before us as we endure the hardships around us.

Finding joy around us

In a broken world the joy we want is sometimes found in what we avoid. No one wants to suffer or sacrifice. No one wants to hurt or feel helpless. No one chooses to give up something for someone else.

So why would we?

This is how God showed his love among us: He sent his one and only Son into the world that we might live through him. 1 John 4:9 (NIV)

Love chooses what is best for others despite what it costs us. Jesus says it is that act of giving away our lives that brings us the most abundant life. We choose to give away what was freely given to us. Love.

Jesus looked upon our world in need and his love couldn't sit by and not act. Compassion is an action. Jesus knew love had to do something. Yes, it would be hard. Yes, it would require all of heaven to raise up what He was about to lay down. But Jesus knew the secret to living was giving. So he gave. To us. For us. Jesus knew that the greatest reward in loving and giving was the joy at the end of the journey knowing His life changed ours. The joy inside Him was greater than what was going on around Him. He knew His earthly life and death would change our lives eternally. The purpose and passion in His mission was what kept him enduring to the end of His mission.

You and I were the joy Jesus was living and dying for. Joy is the abundant outpouring of love pouring out of us.

Joy empowers us to endure all things when love is our motivation.

Many times life requires us to endure hardship. We must go through something we aren't sure we are going to come through. Love is what chooses to endure hardship. Joy is the reward as we endure hard things.

Jesus whispers, "Hang on, the joy that is coming will overcome the pain you are experiencing!" Joy tells us we can do hard things because they become holy things. God is not random. The people we encounter as we walk through life are meant to be part of how we experience God. There are no chance meetings in life. Only chances to change someone else's life. This living to give in love is how we find abundant life. God touches others through us. We are touched by God when we see the joy of our lives intertwining with theirs as God writes a story of beauty we couldn't have dreamed of or decided upon. We experience the greatest joy when we give away the love God has given to us.

God's greatest gift was given to us and for us. When we live and give in that same spirit we will experience a joy set before us that will propel us into places and spaces we never could have imagined. Places where we find the joy we might always have been looking for.

When others find Jesus we will find joy. Joy is not dependent on our current state or condition but rather is a result of what God has done for us, in us and promises to complete through us. We must

iola ★ JOY

look past our present circumstances and toward the reward found in a life motivated by enduring love.

I had no idea that bumpy, dusty road into that obscure village in Africa would lead me to joy. I found what I was looking for when those children found what they needed. Joy, unspeakable joy.

"And the angel said to them, "Fear not, for behold, I bring you good news of great joy that will be for all the people. 11 For unto you is born this day in the city of David a Savior, who is Christ the Lord." Luke 2:10-11 (ESV)

This GREAT joy came to all of us. His love was big enough to save us and humble enough to meet us in our messy, dark, hard moments. Jesus was willing to endure all things for all of us so that we might find the joy of His great love.

Jesus's inward joy for what He loved was far greater than the outward obstacles he would have to endure to get to us. The joy within Him took Him off His Heavenly throne and on to this planet. There was more going on that silent night in Bethlehem than met the eye. Sometimes we overlook the ordinary because we can't see the extraordinary and profound love of God hiding in it.

All of heaven was full of joy as they watched their heavenly prince come to us. I imagine they were jumping for joy knowing we were all about to experience something we had never seen, touched or known before.

Joy is found unexpectedly in moments where love chooses. Joy jumps and plays. Joy is not a denial of hardship but rather a gift in it. Ordinary life offers us the opportunity to find extraordinary joy when we seek love and share love with others.

Jesus is joy. When we have Jesus in us we carry joy around with us. When we love in His name our ordinary lives can become lavish expressions of an enduring and unexplainable love.

I left those children in Africa many years ago, but they have never left my heart. To this day I can't think about joy without remembering those eleven children leaping on that beach and how my heart jumped out of my chest as they experienced God in their joy.

Unexpected. Unexplainable. Undeniable.

The enduring love of Christ had connected us. The power of love had changed us. Unexpected joy had captured us. Finding joy in unexpected places is worth the journey love will take you on.

"I have told you these things so that you will be filled with my joy. Yes, your joy will overflow!" John 15:11

Laura is a writer and speaker. She lives in upstate NY with her husband of 23 years and their six children. Laura's desire is to connect her audience with God. Laura's speaking and writing has inspired and impacted thousands to connect with God over the last 15 years. Laura writes bold, beautiful and brave words that stir your heart. Every word, spoken or written, invites you to live the crazy amazing life of love, hope and faith you were born for. Laura writes and speaks the truth of God's Word passionately. She believes that a girl and the gospel are a powerful force God uses every day to turn ordinary into extraordinary. Laura believes that every woman can live her purpose, pursue her passion and IGNITE the world with the power and love of Jesus Christ.
www.readysetgogirl.com

iola ★ JOY

Go out with Joy

May you know joy insuppressable,
even in your spentness.

May you return with joy,
even when you went out with tears.

We pray you see glitter glimpses of eternity
in the lift of others heads, hearts and lips,

and that you slay the kitchen dance floor
with all your might.

Printed in Great Britain
by Amazon